MYSTRAS

Publishers: George A. Christopoulos, John C. Bastias
Managing Editor: Efi Karpodini-Dimitriadi
Translation: Alison Frantz-Louise Turner
Art Director: Nicos Andricakis
Special Photography: J. Trimis, N. Kontos

MYSTRAS

THE MEDIEVAL CITY AND THE CASTLE

A COMPLETE GUIDE TO THE CHURCHES, PALACES AND THE CASTLE

MANOLIS CHATZIDAKIS
MEMBER OF THE ACADEMY
OF ATHENS

EKDOTIKE ATHENON S.A.
Athens 2001

ISBN 960-213-065-2

Copyright © *1981*

by

EKDOTIKE ATHENON S.A.

1, Vissarionos Street

Athens 106 72, Greece

PRINTED AND BOUND IN GREECE

by

EKDOTIKE HELLADOS S.A.

An affiliated company

8, Philadelphias Street, Athens

CONTENTS

1. General view of Mystras; Mt. Taygetos in the background.

2. *One of the entrances into the Upper Town; the Monemvasia Gate.* ▶

AUTHOR'S PREFACE

More than thirty years have elapsed since the author first wrote a guide to Mystras. In these decades much work has been carried out by the archaeologists successively in charge of the ruins of the byzantine city. All of them were young men at the time of their appointment, and all have worked with enthusiasm not only to excavate, but also to consolidate decaying buildings, to repair the roofs of churches against the penetration of damp and to clean and restore the wall paintings. Indeed, the murals have been so much renovated that they have almost regained their pristine condition.

In these same years the author has widened his acquaintance with byzantine monuments and furthered his knowledge in related fields. But he has never ceased to visit and re-visit Mystra, and to ponder and review the problems posed by its monuments and, naturally, to consider their significance for the art of the epoch they represent. The same problems have occupied the minds of other scholars (see bibliography), and a summary of the conclusions reached by such researches is to be found in this small book.

Manolis Chatzidakis

THE RUINED CITY

As you leave the town of Sparta behind and come closer to the mass of Mount Taygetos, the conical shape of the hill of Mystras gradually becomes visible at its foot. From nearer still, the medieval town which spreads out over the slopes of Taygetos fills your vision, a lacework pattern of ruins. At the very bottom of the slope, behind the defences you see churches, monasteries and the two and three-storeyed houses of the aristocracy: higher up your eye is drawn by the palaces, churches and even more houses, in fact by innumerable dwellings. On the peak of the hill the never conquered castle rears up like an imposing warrior.

Apart from seven churches and the castle, the rest of the buildings are dilapidated and in ruins. As you saunter uphill along the narrow streets or wander through the arched lanes, curiosity compels you to glance into the empty houses. Brushing against the walls — for you can touch both sides of the lane with outstretched arms — you are overwhelmed by the forlornness of the dead city which you feel around you. The life and bustle of the medieval centuries have petrified into the absolute silence of death, and the stillness is disturbed by nothing more noisy than the swoop of a hawk. The stones, the walls, the arches and the domes continue to stand in mute existence, and as they crumble and weather away, they take with them what remains of the labour and the skill of the builder and the remnants of the beliefs and feelings of the people who gave life to them, in other words of those who created the form inside the space. As you wander from one church to the next, admiring these buildings which were splendid by the standards of their own time and even today are amongst the most brilliant and shining examples of the medieval builders' work, you are bathed in a dim religious light, and your soul is uplifted by their symmetrical dimensions harmoniously matched to

the size of man. Every church in Mystras had its own individual form; altogether they are subjected with grace to the canons of classical simplicity, proportion and balance. Inside, on the surface of the walls of the arches and apses, religion narrates in pictures the Passion of its God and the sufferings of its saints and, in symbolic representations, affirms its dogmatic quintessence. Apart from the religious tone of these depictions, the pious artists who executed them somehow convey directly to us their own feeling for form, for colour and for rhythmic movement. The more you familiarize yourself with their language, the deeper you penetrate into their era; the more you experience their fanaticism for their art and feel the fluctuations of its moods, the more you come to understand the diverse tendencies and appreciate the opposing ideological beliefs that divided them, until you realize with awe that you live in their own era and have acquired a consciousness of the value of the culture which flourished on this rock of the Morea simultaneously with the death agony of an Empire.

Scrambling up the uneven path to the castle, you can hardly fail to recall the many hardened warriors who fought here to protect hellenism from the repeated raids of the Franks, Albanians and Turks. You feel immensely moved when you recollect that here the inhabitants, even in the darkest hours of the Byzantine Empire, found the courage to fight for freedom.

From the summit of the watch tower you see the silvery plain of the Eurotas, and at your feet stretches the ruined town, silent as if sunk in a reverie of the past. Down below in the palaces lived the Frankish princesses, wives of the Greek Despots, all of who died so young — the sad-eyed sorrowing ladies of this foreign land. In one of the aristocratic mansions lived and taught the detractor of Christian Byzantium, Plethon, also known as Gemistos, the "wisest of the philosophers" and the glory of Mystras.

3. *Partial view of the ruined city of Mystras; the castle and the palaces.*

4. *Another view of the ruined city of Mystras.*

HISTORY

LOCATION AND SETTING

Four miles north-west of the modern town of Sparta, a steep foothill, cut off from the main massif, rises on the northern slopes of Mt. Taygetos. The visitor approaching Taygetos from Sparta first sees the outline of the hill and then, more gradually, distinguishes the medieval city on its slopes. Low down, churches, monasteries and houses rise from behind the walls; higher up is the palace, surrounded by more churches and tightly clustered houses; dominant on the summit stands the citadel.

Both its natural features and its central position in the heart of the Morea (the Peloponnese) determined the history of Mystras. The natural site is exceptionally strong and easily defensible. The summit of the hill stands 621 m. above sea-level (about 2070 feet), and it is inaccessible from the south and south-west, where rocky cliffs fall away abruptly into a ravine. Its other slopes are also sufficiently steep to provide defensive cover for the approaches. Moreover, the hill controls the entrance to "the gorge of the Melingi", a deep river bed which leads up into the inner fastnesses of Taygetos, a region inhabited in medieval times by Slavic tribes, the Melingi.

Mystras was first made into a stronghold by the Franks; it was later taken over as a focal point in the Byzantine defence of the Morea against the Turks. For two hundred years, it was also one of the last outposts of Byzantine civilisation. Its development as one of the most important cities of the Morea was much facilitated by the contours of the hill. The summit is a broad plateau, which made possible the erection of a citadel. Lower down, on the northern slope, is a second flat space large enough to hold the palace and the central square (the *phoros* of the Byzantines).

Medieval Mystras dates from the building of the castle in 1249 A.D. by William II of Villehardouin, French Prince of Achaia from 1245 to 1278. It is probable that the settlement outside the citadel, next to the palace and above the open square, was established about the same time. This original settlement includes the oldest houses in Mystras, the eastern wing of the palace and a part of the little palace. This first settlement was protected by a wall which originated on the west side of the castle, skirted the steep northern edge of the plateau, then turned east and passed above the later Monastery of the Pantanassa. Two fortified gates guarded the only entrances to the walled town: the Monemvasia Gate to the east, and the Nauplia Gate to the west. The two gates were connected by a central street which ran through the main square. On the south side of the square was the Monastery of Christ Zoodotes, probably the present St. Sophia, built about the middle of the 14th century to serve as the palace church.

Most of the churches lie outside the circuit of the first defences. On the lower northern slopes of the hill are the two churches dedicated to SS. Theodore and the *Hodegetria* (also called the *Aphendiko*), which together constitute the monastery of the *Brontochion*. These are amongst the earliest churches of Mystras, dating from the end of the 13th to the beginning of the 14th centuries. Further to the east stands the *Metropolis,* or Cathedral, built in the last decades of the 13th century, and dedicated to St Demetrios. Later, the Monastery of the *Peribleptos* was constructed against the rocks of the south-east slope. The church of the

Evangelistria, which lies between the *Metropolis* and the *Brontochion,* dates from the end of the 14th century.

As the city grew and houses as well as churches and monasteries were built outside the walls, it became necessary to surround this area with a second fortification wall. The new settlement was known as the Middle, or the Lower, Town, while the older settlement was referred to as the Town or the Upper Town. In addition to the buildings we have already noted, the Middle Town includes certain large houses said to have belonged to distinguished families such as the Lascarides, the Frangopouloi and others. During the 15th century, the period of Mystras' greatest prosperity, the whole slope was inhabited, and the monasteries, originally remote from the city, were then surrounded by houses and protected by the walls. But expansion continued beyond the second wall, and a new settlement was formed on the opposite bank of the river, the Outer Town, inhabited, at least during the Turkish Occupation by the Jewish population.

Much of this medieval city is still standing. The remains include the castle, large sections of the fortifications, the monasteries and churches mentioned above, the palace, hundreds of ruined houses, and many cobbled streets and arched lanes. It should be remembered that the site was inhabited until about 1830, and many of the ruined houses are Turkish. From the early travellers, we learn that the Turks built few mosques or other public buildings. They preferred to make use of the buildings already there, and transformed churches to serve as their own places of worship, as they did, for example, at St. Sophia. Mystras has preserved its byzantine character to our own time.

MYSTRAS BEFORE 1249

We have no information about the history of Mystras before the foundation of the castle in 1249. Inscriptions and fragments of ancient marbles have been found built into the walls of the buildings of the town, but research has not yet revealed any trace of pre-classical or classical habitation in the immediate vicinity. A Roman sarcophagus, carved with representations of maenads, griffins and a sphinx is to be found now in the court of the *Metropolis.* For centuries it served to catch the waters from a spring at the Fountain of Marmara, so called from this monument. A similar sarcophagus, decorated with Erotes carrying garlands, was found about a hundred years ago near another spring, but it has subsequently disappeared. However, since no traces of ancient buildings have been found in this area, the presence of these and other ancient marbles in Mystras is to be explained by the history of the town itself.

The builders of Mystras brought much of their building material, both dressed blocks and carved fragments, from the ruined churches and houses of Sparta, the medieval Lacedaemonia, abandoned in favour of the new town. In the same way, earlier, the medieval Spartans had built their houses out of materials from ancient Sparta; and later, when the modern town was founded in 1831 by King Otho, its inhabitants pilfered material from the ruins of Mystras. Every time a new city was founded, materials ready to hand were taken from the older settlement. This continuous re-use accounts for the presence of carved decoration of the 10th to 12th centuries as well as still more ancient remains in the churches of Mystras.

Even before William of Villehardouin built his castle, the locality was known as *Myzithras.* That name, somewhat abbreviated, preserved first by the capital of the Principate and later by that of the Despotat, has continued in use until today. It was probably called after some landowner of the region whose name or whose trade was that of "cheese-maker", *myzithras*. Whether or not the site was inhabited immediately preceding the construction of the castle,we do not know. It has been suggested that the Metropolis existed before 1249, but the arguments are neither persuasive or conclusive. There is no archaeological or epigraphical evidence for the other buildings, but in all probability there was no important settlement on the site before the construction of the citadel.

MYSTRAS — A FRANKISH CASTLE (1249-1262)

The building of the castle of Mystras in 1249 marks the final phase of the Frankish effort to establish the sovereignty over the Peloponnese which they had obtained in 1204, following the capture of Constantinople and the division of the Byzantine Empire amongst the participants in the Fourth Crusade.

The attempts of Geoffrey I and Geoffrey II of Villehardouin to spread the hegemony of the Principate of Achaia over the entire Morea had been hindered by the hostility not only of the Slavic tribes, but also of the Greek population, both feudal rulers and common people. In 1248, however, with the help of the Venetians, William II was succesful in blockading and reducing the coastal fortres of Monemvasia. This castle was the key to the defence of the entire southeast Peloponnese, which included the regions of Laconia, Mani and the Slavic districts on Mt. Taygetos. Its fall gave the ruler of the Principate of Achaia control over the whole Peloponnese, except for a few cities held by the Venetians. In order to consolidate his conquests, William sought and "found a remarkable hill, a fragment of a mountain", and there in 1249 he built a fortress and "called it Myzithras because they shouted it thus, and he made it into a glorious castle and a great *chateau fort*" (Chronicle of the Morea, lines 2990-2991). At Great Maina on the Mani peninsula he built another fortress, from which repeated assaults on the Slavic populations forced them into submission. External complications, however, brought the Principate of Achaia into conflict with the Greek Empire of Nicaea; the Battle of Pelagonia (1259), when William himself was taken prisoner, ended in a disastrous defeat for the Franks. In 1262, in order to pay his own ransom, William ceded the fortresses of Monemvasia, the Great Maina and "third and more beautiful the castle of Myzithras" to the Greeks (Chron. Mor. line 4331).

Thus the Greeks obtained a stable base in the Peloponnese not only for military operations, but also for cultural expansion. This base they were not to lose until the Turkish Conquest.

MYSTRAS AS THE SEAT OF A BYZANTINE MILITARY GOVERNOR (1262-1348)

After 1262, the Greek district of the Morea was governed by a Byzantine general, appointed annually, whose headquarters were at Mystras. Nevertheless, despite the acquisition of the town by the Greeks, attempts to regain it were made by the Franks and for a time there was continuous, though inconclusive, fighting.

This brought one positive result. After the battle of Makryplagi in 1264, the inhabitants of Sparta, who suffered most from the uncertain conditions, finally moved to the shelter of the fortress. Their migration was the nucleus of the first domestic settlement in the "region of Myzithras", and, because it was followed soon afterwards by a short period of peace beginning in 1289, it provided the first impulse to development. The last decades of the 13th century witnessed the expansion of Mystras from village to city. The Metropolis was built, monasteries were founded, and the palace enlarged. The increased population spurred the shaping of a cultural life, and leaders in fields other than military began to emerge. One such, the Protosyngelos Pachomios, was the co-founder of the Monastery of SS. Theodore shortly before 1269. Later, about 1310, he built the church of the Hodegetria (the Aphendiko) in the Monastery of the Brontochion. Pachomios held the office of Abbot for life, and under his auspices the monastery became an important centre of political and cultural activity. He also founded a library and assisted needy scholars.

At the same time the seat of the bishopric of Lacedaemonia was moved to Mystras. The Metropolis, dedicated to St. Demetrios, was built in the years following 1264, probably by the metropolite Eugenios.

Because of the efforts of such men, the importance of Mystras increased rapidly. After 1308, the office of governor ceased to be an annual appointment, and become instead a life tenure. The young Katakouzenos (1308-1316) was the first holder of the title on these terms, and the improvement in the efficiency of the office was both marked and immediate. He was succeeded by the energetic Andronicos Palaiologos Asan (1316-1321) who extended his sway as far as Akova and Karytaina.

MYSTRAS AS THE CAPITAL OF THE DESPOTAT (1348-1460)
The Katakouzenoi (1348-1384)

By the middle of the fourteenth century the Peloponnese was of considerable political standing in the Byzantine Empire, despite the fact that social and economic conditions were bad. The region was not only exposed to the incursions of both Franks and Turks, but it was also torn by incessant and destructive internal struggles. It was this state of affairs which forced the new Emperor, John VI Katakouzenos, to send his second son, Manuel, to the Morea to rule with authority to do what he thought best to stabilize the situation. This marked the creation of the Despotat of the Morea, a government more autonomous than before, but bound directly to the Emperor in a clear-cut feudal relationship.

Manuel Katakouzenos was an able man; within a short time he succeeded in putting an end to the civil wars and in suppressing the repeated insurrections of local rulers. The causes of these revolts were two-fold: sometimes they were a protest against the imposition of levies for the fortification of the Despotat, and at other times they were the result of instigation on the part of the Palaiologoi. After the Palaiologoi had succeeded in dethroning John VI as Emperor of Byzantium, they naturally sought to expel his sons from their advantageous positions.

During Manuel's lengthy rule Mystras enjoyed a certain degree of peace and prosperity. About 1350 Manuel built the Monastery of Zoodotes which should be identified with St. Sophia. At about the same time, the abbot Kyprianos constructed the north and south chapels of the Aphendiko, and the church of the Peribleptos was deccorated with wall paintings.

Manuel married Isabella, daughter of Guy de Lusignan, King of Lesser Armenia. Her name is inscribed on an epistyle now in the Museum of the Metropolis.

Manuel was succeeded by his brother Matthew (1380-1383), whose son and heir, Demetrius, (1383-1384), brought the rule of the Katakouzenoi to an end by his attempt to sever the dependency of the Despotat on Constantinople. The Emperor John V Palaiologos despatched an army under the command of his son Theodore which crushed the revolt. Thus the Palaiologoi banished their opponents, and Theodore ruled as Despot.

The Palaiologoi (1384-1460)

The rule of the Palaiologue dynasty was characterized firstly by an even closer relationship between the Despotat and the capital than before, and secondly by an expansionist policy, so that the power of the Despotat was extended to include almost all the Peloponnese. The consequence was the enhanced importance of Mystras in both the political and the cultural life of the Empire, despite the fact that peace was not absolute. In addition to the external threats from the Turks, Navarrese and Venetians, there were frequent fratricidal conflicts within the imperial family. Furthermore relations between the central authorities and the feudal lords were often strained. All these evils were exacerbated by economic difficulties, by the infiltration of foreign economic interests, and by the establishment of the Albanians as a separate national element.

The population of the Peloponnese at this time was composed mainly of Greeks, but there still existed small tightly-knit groups of Slavs, and a considerable number of Albanians who had begun to migrate to the Morea during the preceding period. There were also a number of Jews. However, the dominant position, both political and cultural, was securely held by Greeks. Not only had all foreigners, of different races and less developed civilisations, gradually begun to become hellenised, but even the Frankish colonists had adapted themselves to the life of their subjects, and had become accustomed to speak Greek. An example of their language is preserved in the *Chronicle of the Morea,* from which a few passages have already been quoted. This poem, of about 9000 lines, is a Greek variation of a metric chronicle written in French, Italian and Aragonese. An important source for the history of the period, it was probably compiled by an anti-Greek half-breed about the middle of the 14th century in the popular (demotic) language. Nevertheless, the Franks were not without influence on Greek life. For political reasons, all the Despots married Frankish princesses, and these connections explain certain characteristics of the art of Mystras.

It is important to stress that the forced co-existence of Greeks and Franks and the incessant conflicts that arose from this had generated a strong nationalistic feeling, especially in the lower strata of the Greek population. This became evident when, because he was under Turkish military pressure, Theodore I Palaiologos (1384-1407), ceded Mystras to the Knights of St John of Rhodes in return for a reward. In 1402 the representatives of the Knights appeared to claim the city, but the population rose against them, and their lives were saved only by the intervention of the bishop. Theodore was obliged to revoke his deed. The attitude of the feudal lords, however, was in complete contrast to this popular national feeling, for they never hesitated to form alliances either with the Turks or with the Venetians whenever their privileged position was threatened. This happened in the case mentioned above; it occurred again with Mamonas of Monemvasia, and was repeated later during the civil wars between the Palaiologos brothers.

Theodore I Palaiologos, brother of the Emperor Manuel II, was succeeded by his nephew Theodore II (1407-1443). Manuel himself took great interest in the Despotat, and lived there at two different periods. He was especially interested in the construction of the fortifications of Hexamilion near Corinth. He aroused much discontent both amongst the local rulers and amongst the populace by the heavy taxation he levied for the project. Despite his efforts, the fortifications did not prevent the Turks from reaching Mystras in 1423, ravaging the Peloponnese and taking prisoners before they withdrew.

By about 1429, however, as a result of the military and diplomatic successes of Theodore and his brother John VIII, the new Emperor, the entire Peloponnese was firmly in Greek hands with the exception of a few Venetian coastal possessions (Methone, Corone and Nauplia). At that time a second Despotat was established in the Morea with its capital at Glarentza. It was ruled by Theodore's brother, Constantine.

Constantine followed a dynamic and, to some extent, a Panhellenic policy. He aimed to extend his domain from the Morea to include the whole of mainland Greece. Although civil wars and the increasing Turkish power prevented him from realising his plan, the Morea remained a flourishing centre of Byzantine civilisation and a firm outpost of the Empire.

In 1430, a third Despotat was established under the rule of Thomas Palaiologos, brother of the two other Despots. His seat was at Kalavryta, which he later exchanged with Constantine for Glarentza. Soon, however, dynastic disputes over the succession to the throne in Constantinople brought the brothers into conflict, which was sometimes open and armed, at other times concealed and diplomatic. After a succession of agreements, it was finally settled that Constantine should be Despot of Mystras (1443-1449), where he remained until he went to Constantinople to be crowned as Emperor, a title which he was the last to hold.

In 1446, the Turks once more invaded the Peloponnese. The slaughter and capture of prisoners was halted only by the payment of tribute by the Greek Despots to the Sultan Mourat. In 1453, the Albanian settlers in the Morea revolted against the Greek Despots Thomas and Demetrios, roused to this action not by the news of the Fall of Constantinople alone, but further incited by the ousted Katakouzenoi, and strengthened by the power which the Albanians themselves had acquired within the Despot's army.

Without the help of the Sultan Mohammed II, the Palaiologoi would not have been able to suppress the revolt. From this time on, their hold on power became more and more tenuous. To make matters worse, the brothers once again took up arms against each other, for they were on opposite sides in the ideological struggles which marked the last years of the Empire. Demetrios at Mystras, like George Scholaris at Constantinople, was well-disposed to the Turks and disliked the Franks, while Thomas at Patras, like Bessarion, sought help from the Pope and the western leaders against the Turks.

This state of anarchy in the Peloponnese, which was not discouraged by the western powers, was brought to an end by the arrival of Mohammed II with a large army. On May 30 1460 Demetrios handed over Mystras, and attached himself to the court of the Sultan, while Thomas fled to Italy. The conquest of the rest

5. The Emperor Manuel II Palaiologos in a miniature from a manuscript.
(Paris, Bibliothèque Nationale).

of the Peloponnese was greatly hindered by the strong resistance of the inhabitants, and it was not completed until July 1461. With its submission, however, the history of the Greek Despotat of the Morea ended.

Mystras, both castle and town, was a creation of the last centuries of the Byzantine Empire. Even now it presents a complete picture of the byzantine city state as it developed in the difficult years which followed the Frankish conquest of the Morea. Many castles, and around them small townships, many of which had only a short life, grew up in this period, for example Nikli, Mouchli, Veligosti, Vostitza, Andravida, Geraki and numerous other foundations of either Frankish or Byzantine origin. All these reveal the importance attached to the Peloponnese in these centuries as the cross-roads and furthest-flung point of contact between Franks and Byzantines. For the Byzantines, the Peloponnese was one of the few areas of the Empire which had close and continuing connections with Constantinople, linked to the capital by bonds of political and intellectual dependence.

Mystras was the soul and centre of the Greek Peloponnese. For the period it was a large town, and the security of its hillside site, strengthened by the two concentric sets of fortifications, encouraged the building of the palaces, aristocratic mansions, monasteries, the metropolitan and many other churches. The citadel, towering above all, helped the "God-guarded country of Myzithra" to maintain its independence. As time passed, the small Greek state which had grown up around the Frankish *Chateau-fort* of Villehardouin before the end of the 13th century, became stronger, and its relations at every level with Constantinople became closer.

Mystras was also the seat of the Metropolite of Lacedaemonia. It was frequently visited by outstanding political and ecclesiastical figures from Constantinople such as the metropolite Nikephoros Moschopoulos both connoisseur and intellectual. Other artists, connoisseurs and intellectuals lived in Mystras; for example, Pachomios, Protosyngelos and abbot of the great monastery of the Brontochion. Early on, Mystras became a centre for thinkers, scribes and copyists. After 1400, the figure of George Plethon Gemistos the "awe-inspiring philosopher", founder of a School, dominated the scene. His presence coincided with the love for classical literature and philosophy which was first manifested at the end of the 14th century and remained a burning flame to the end. At the same time magnificent works of architecture were built, magnificent not so much because of their size and the quality of the materials, but because of the harmonic coupling of local plain and unaffected good taste, experienced in the use of stone and brick, with the more decorative morphology of the School of Constantinople, experienced in the construction of stoas, big narthexes and the use of the external arch-like decoration. All these buildings are embellished with glorious frescoes which adorn the interior walls from top to bottom like a multi-coloured fabric.

AFTER 1460

Naturally, during the Turkish domination, Mystras ceased to occupy the supreme position which it had hitherto held. From time to time it was the seat of a Pasha, and it was the established seat of a vilayet which comprised 118 villages in its district. The Venetians made a vain attempt to capture the castle in 1464; the tyrant of Rimini, Sigismund Malatesta, managed to penetrate the town. In 1687, the Venetian Morosini succeeded in capturing the city. Although the seafaring

6. Engraving of Mystras in the 17th century; Athens, Gennadeion Library.

Venetians naturally transferred the government of the Province of Laconia to Monemvasia, Mystras remained a flourishing commercial centre thanks to its silk industry, and its population reached 42,000. The enclosure of the Peribleptos dates from 1714. In 1715 the Turks once more captured the citadel and used it as a base for military operations against the inhabitants of the Mani.

During the Orloff uprising of 1770, Mystras was liberated for a few months, only to suffer a savage attack from the Albanians, who put it to fire and sword and ruled it for ten years.

Travellers at the beginning of the 19th century found more houses in ruins than standing, and noted that the production of silk had fallen to one seventh of the former output.

With the Greek War of Independence, Mystras was liberated once more, although in 1825 it was again burned, this time by the Egyptians led by Ibrahim. From then on it ceased to have any importance. The foundation of modern Sparta by King Otho in 1831 marked the final demise of the town. The distinguished families moved to the new capital, and others descended to New Mystras, a well wooded village built in the plain. A few inhabitants remained in the Lower Town but they have recently been removed from there.

21

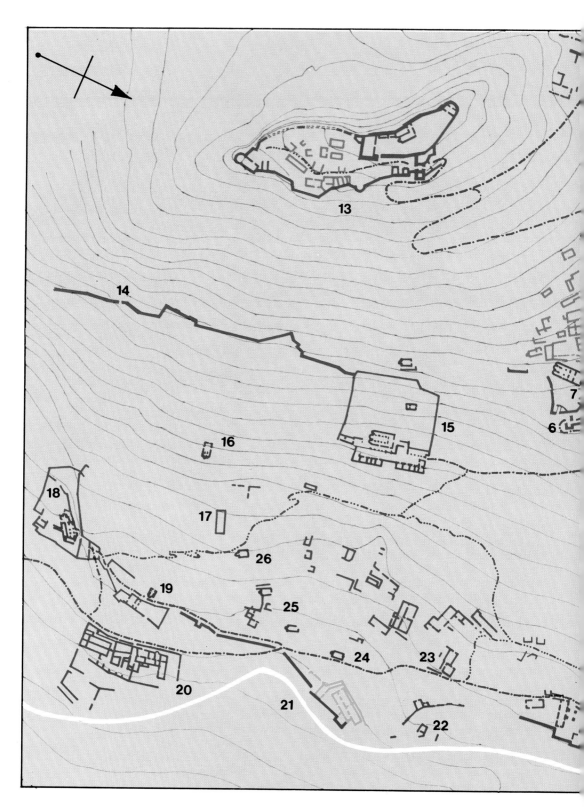

PLAN OF MYSTRAS

1. The Main Entrance

2. The Metropolis

3. The Evangelistria

4. SS. Theodore

5. Hodegetria-Aphendiko

6. The Monemvasia Gate

7. St. Nicholas

8. The Palace of the Despots and the central square

9. The Nauplia Gate

10. The Upper entrance to the citadel

11. St. Sophia

12. The Little Palace

13. The Castle

14. The Mavroporta

15. The Pantanassa

16. The Taxiarchs

17. The House of Phrangopoulos

18. The Peribleptos

19. St. George

20. The House of Krevatas, 18th century

21. Marmara — the entrance

22. Aï Yannakis

23. The House of Lascaris

24. St. Christopher

25. Ruined house

26. St. Kyriake

7. The Metropolis (St. Demetrios) east side with the later bell-tower.

THE MONUMENTS OF MYSTRAS

For the visitor who has only a short time at his disposal, it is best to visit first the monuments of the Lower Town. The modern automobile road leads to the main entrance to the old city through the outer wall. The first church to the right is the Metropolis, entered through a small door giving onto the narrow street. After visiting the Metropolis, the best plan is to continue on this street in the same direction, passing Byzantine houses on the left, and proceeding to the little church of the Evangelistria. From there, the road goes on to the churches of SS. Theodore and finally to the Aphendiko.

Access to the Town or the Upper Town is gained through the Monemvasia Gate, from which the street leads to the Palace and thence to St. Sophia. To visit the citadel, continue along the same street, and then follow the road which begins at the uppermost gate in the wall. Another entrance is above St. Sophia. From there one reaches the peak of the hill or alternatively, one can take this route in reverse, descending from the citadel to St. Sophia, the Palace and from there to SS. Theodore and the Metropolis. Then take the narrow road leading uphill to the Pantanassa, or continue in the same direction eastwards to reach the Peribleptos.

The Upper Town includes, besides many smaller Byzantine houses, the great mansion which lies east of St. Sophia and, a little below that, St. Nicholas, a big church of the Turkish period. From the Pantanassa, where the path to the Upper Town ends, another track leads to the Peribleptos, passing through the ruins of chapels and Byzantine houses. Amongst the fallen masonry the so-called House of the Phrangopouloi can be distinguished. From the Peribleptos a road leads straight down to Marmara.

It is useful to know that the Peribleptos is well lit only in the morning, since it is built against the rock face. For the other churches the time of day when they are best visited makes less difference.

THE METROPOLIS

The complex of buildings which makes up the Metropolis lies along the northern inner edge of the outer wall. There are two entrances; a small one from the old narrow street which runs at the higher level on the south side, and a second, later and more imposing, from the western court. The older entrance leads straight to the *gynaikonitis,* or women's gallery, which is at the level of the street, and from there to a narrow covered staircase on the left which descends to the western court. On the wall of the stairway, almost opposite the door is a metrical inscription which records the dedication of the church by Nikephoros, *proedros* of Crete and metropolite of Lacedaemonia, and his brother Aaron. The date of the inscription is 1291-92. Another inscription on the lintel over the main entrance to the church, adjures the reader to remember the founder Nikephoros. An account of his work in the Metropolis of Lacedaemonia, dated 1311-12, is scratched on the first column on our right as we enter the church. It informs us that he "built this church", reconstructed the mills at Magoula, and planted olive trees and a garden there, and bought the houses near the church which belonged to Eugenios the Chartophylax (later bishop of Amyclae). It ends with the warning that whoever dares to take any of these properties away from the church will bring down on himself the curses of the 318 Fathers as well as Nikephoros' own.

This energetic and learned bishop has been identified with Nikephoros

8. *The buildings of the Metropolis and, left, the Evangelistria, seen from above.*

Moschopoulos, a titulary metropolite of Crete (*proedros*). He was not without influence on the political and ecclesiastical affairs of his time, was a well known transcriber of manuscripts and possessor of an important library. He was elected to the see of Lacedaemonia between 1286-1289, and he held this office until 1315. Nikephoros probably did not build anything of the Metropolis other than the narthex. The main church was erected by a bishop before him, probably by the Eugenios who is portrayed in the diaconicon. The wall paintings in the church are probably also connected with the work of an earlier bishop, Theodosius (1272).

Later bishops have also left records of the property and privileges they obtained for the Metropolis: Loukas of Sougdaia scratched his record on the third column on the left in 1330, and Neilos his achievements of 1339, 1340 and 1341 on the third on the right.

ARCHITECTURE

The church has not preserved its original form. Nikephoros built it as a basilica, the traditional style of cathedral churches such as we find in the metropolitan churches of Kalabaka, Serres, Ochrida and others.

The basilica was divided into three aisles by two rows of three columns each, the central aisle being much higher than those on either side. Originally, all three aisles were barrel-vaulted. Later, probably in the 15th century, an insensitive and vain-glorious bishop who has left his name everywhere, Matthew, tried to adapt the basilica to the plan of the Aphendiko and the Pantanassa by tearing the roof down to the level of the present interior cornice with the deep carving. On the west side the cornice bears the inscription "Matthew Bishop of Lacedaemonia Founder". He added a women's gallery in an upper storey consisting of four groined vaults and five domes. The central and largest dome is supported on four piers which in turn rest on the original colonnade. Thus the church today is a basilica on the ground floor and a cross-in-square church on the upper storey. This combination is unusual in Byzantine architecture, although there are two examples at Mystras, the earlier and more successful being the Aphendiko. In the Metropolis the modification was made rather ineptly, its haphazard proportions leaving a ponderous impression. The original interior decoration suffered badly. Matthew treated the frescoes of Nikephoros just as the Roman remodeller of the theatre of Dionysos on the slopes of the Acropolis in Athens treated the frieze of the scene building: he decapitated the figures. Thus all the figures in the cycle of the life of Christ depicted on the south side of the central aisle are headless.
The original height of the church and the arrangement of the central aisle can still be seen clearly high up within the central apse. Closely spaced windows admitted abundant light to the church, and between the windows the figures of standing prophets were depicted.

The exterior of the church is simple, but the two building periods can be clearly differentiated. The most interesting part is the eastern end, where the apses belong almost entirely to the first period. This whole side, from window sills upwards, is characterized by the careful wall construction in *cloisonné masonry*, a style which distinguishes the churches of the Helladic School from the second half of the 10th century on. Each carefully dressed block of stone, surrounded by a row of bricks, gives the impression of austere calculation, in which there is no element of chance, while the interplay of warm colours — the golden hue of the stone in the sunlight and the red of the terracotta — is harmonious and restful to the eye. The beautiful series of closely spaced windows is emphasized by a row of brick saw-tooth ornament below. The same decoration crowns the three-sided apses and, in a double row, frames the arch of the central aisle beneath the saddle roof. The tympanum of this arch is adorned with a two-lobed window between two sculptured slabs built into the wall; one is carved in relief with animals and stylized vines (10th-11th century) and the other, contemporary with the church, bears only a mosaic circle. Both plaques have been hollowed out in the centre to hold a decorative faience plate. The monotony of the walls above the side apses is broken by two white rectangular slabs with a red mosaic circle.

On the south side the ground rises almost to the middle of the wall, so that only Matthew's addition is visible. It may be reckoned to begin from the sculptured band upwards. This side is carelessly built; *cloisonné masonry* is used only in the main walls, while on the arches the bricks are indicated by paint on the plaster.

A belfry, resembling a heavy tower, built on a former chapel, was added to the south side after Nikephoros' death (1316).

The west facade is adorned with an arcature of three piers, covered with a triple barrel vault. This arcade, ill adjusted to the facade, added by Matthew, lends a certain heavy dignity to the church. It originally had three arches and four pilasters, but at the left end of the porch Matthew added later a small episcopal hall which disturbs the disposition of the original facade. Next to the windows Matthew's monogram is displayed in painted bricks.

The church has links with Thessalonica through the saint to whom it is dedicated. Its main characteristics, however, the smooth triple apses, the barrel-vaulted side aisles, the small number of windows, the masonry and above all the classical feeling, place it among the most important monuments of the Helladic School, rooted in the ancient traditions of the land. The 15th century addition, however, reflects the strong influences which came to Mystras from Constantinople with the building of the Aphendiko.

On the north side of the church, the court in its present form, with porches and colonnades on three sides, dates from the Turkish Occupation. An inscription records the construction of the western range in 1754 by the bishop Ananias Lampardis of Dimitsana, martyr priest killed by the Turks in 1760.

SCULPTURED DECORATION

The decoration of the church is completed by the sculpture and the pavement.

The sculpture lacks unity of either style or period, since most of it was brought to Mystras from elsewhere and is only re-used here. Thus the four westernmost column capitals are Early Christian in style, bearing spear-shaped leaves and acanthus, while the two easternmost are coarse imitations of the same theme. The iconostasis has been built up from many pieces, and displays a wealth of sculptured decoration of various styles and periods, none of which is later than the 12th century. It must, however, have taken its present form in the 18th century or even later. Particularly worthy of attention is one of the door jambs of the prothesis; the flutings form knots, and on its wider upper part is a centaur in relief, carved following a simple popular conception. A similar mixture of styles may be observed in the north doorway, where perhaps only the door-frame is contemporary with the construction of the building.

The cornice of the central aisle, with its rinceaux or running vine ornament carved deeply in the soft limestone, belongs to the period of Matthew's activities. The parapet of the women's gallery is made up of slabs carved at different periods and of mediocre quality.

There are two interesting shrines (*proskynetaria*) on the faces of the piers of the sanctuary which frame the original fresco-icons of Christ and the Virgin, standing. Each consists of a projecting semi-circular arch decorated with drilled acanthus leaves, and a rectangular field decorated with geometric designs in red marble inlay. Within the field were two hemispherical bosses, now broken. Such frames are typical of the 13th and 14th centuries, but Bishop Matthew complemented them by adding an ugly cornice and two sills and each bears his monogram.

Outside, on the south wall, is a narrow frieze with examples of sculpture of many different periods and styles. It seems that here too the old churches of Sparta furnished the architects of Mystras with ready made material.

A relief of slab bearing the double-headed eagle of the Palaiologoi is embedded in the floor below the dome. It is not earlier than Matthew's reconstruction, and may even be as late as the period of the Turkish Occupation. Also of Matthew's period are three or four sections in which light-coloured tesserae among dark form rather crude geometric linear designs. Their crudity is accentuated by the fact that in the same pavement fragments of the earliest decoration have survived, of marble inlay flawlessly executed.

THE MUSEUM

The museum is housed in the two-storey west wing of the northern courtyard of the Metropolis. The ground floor is given over to sculptures from the various churches and from excavations of the town of Mystras. These include architectural components, capitals, closure slabs, epistyles from iconostases, divider windows, parts of door frames, as well as devotional relief panels, floor plaques and inscriptions. There are some interesting pieces among the epistyles; for example, one from the Pantanassa with a carefully executed, complex vegetal pattern of Western origin. Others worth noting are the haut relief, also from the Pantanassa, with a symbolic portrayal of St. John the Evangelist -as an eagle clutching the Gospel in its talons- and two fragments from another epistyle bearing the monogram and coat of arms of Isabelle de Lusignan, wife of the Despot Manuel Cantacuzenos (Kantakouzenos). Two slabs with the monogram of the Kantakouzenoi have also been preserved, and a piece from a large cross has a dedicatory inscription by a certain Joseph Armenios from Greater Armenia. Some of the sculptures from the paleochristian and middle Byzantine periods were originally from Sparta and were brought to Mystras either before the Turkish Conquest, when they would have been re-used in the churches, or in more recent years. Into this category falls a round marble plaque showing an eagle attacking a hare framed by a decorative floral border, an example of craftsmanship of the 11th to 12th centrury.

Local technique is at its best and most genuine in the arched shrines. Fragments of two or three of these have been preserved, and one —depicting. Christ Enthroned— has remained intact. In this piece, the artist employed a variety, of techniques. While the body and halo are represented in low relief, the folds in the robes, the hair and the facial features are indicated merely by

9. The Metropolis; the exo-narthex with the later colonnade.

deep incised lines. On the other hand, the base of the frame and the throne are done in champlevé, a technique borrowed from enamelwork, and the background of the footrest would gave been covered with a dark coloured material. Finally, the crowning portion of the frame bears a design based on a pattern of drilled holes. This type of folk art is representative of the indigenous work of the 14th and 15th century, in which traditional wisdom was expressed without any allusion to Classicism, but with a certain naive display of skill.

In the small courtyard behind the main hall there are several capitals arranged on top of columns as well as a few inscriptions in Hebrew. The first floor of the museum contains miniatures, pottery, coins and fragments from frescoes that were found during the excavations at Mystras and Sparta. In the showcase where the miniatures are displayed, among the Byzantine and Venetian coins, simple pieces of jewellery — earrings, rings, brooches — and various other finds, some things stand out, such as the fragment of a bone comb, a talisman carved out of steatite with busts of saints depicted on both sides, and bronze oil lamp bases in the form of animals. Particulary noteworthy is the spherical bronze censer with the large, flat, perforated handle which was found in a tomb in the Lower City and dates from the 14th-15th century. Similar censers are in collections in Greece — the Benaki Museum, Meteora — and in Yugoslavia.

The pieces of silk fabric and the plait — exhibited in a separate case — were found in a tomb in the northern arcade of St. Sophia and must have belonged to one of the noblewomen of Mystras. Other cases contain pottery and sherds of the late Byzantine era. The majority have the typical yellow of green glaze and are decorated with incised animal figures or geometric patterns. Here two pieces that were unearthed recently during the excavations of a three apsed Byzantine church in Sparta deserve special mention. One is the glass with the feet and a hare engraved on the outside, the other a red clay pitcher with a spiral decoration traced on its rounded portions. Monumental painting is represented by the fragments of frescoes which were uncovered during excavations of the various chapels at Mystras. Two of these — a head of the Virgin from a painting of the Birth of Christ and the head of an apostle from a painting of the Ascension — were taken from the chapel of St. Paraskevi in the Upper City and date from the first half of the 14th century. Belonging to the same period are two fragments with heads of female saints from the chapel of St. Anne in the Lower City, Slightly later (mid 14th century) are the head of the Prophet Elijah and the bust of St. Peter from the chapel of St. Christopher.

Among the post-Byzantine icons on exhibit, two stand out: St. John Chrysostomos enthroned, a work of the Cretan artist Theodoros Poulakis, and Christ and the Apostles, signed by the painter Victoros. The latter follows the icnographic formula for depicting Christ' s words: «I am the vine, you are the branches». Also on display in this room is a 14th century marble plaque portraying the Ascension of Alexander the Great, from the floor of the Peribleptos. The carving is in champlevé, and both the decoration and technique reflect a strong Moslem influence. The roughness of the background indicates that the empty spaces may have been filled with some coloured material.

10. The Metropolis; the west side of the exo-narthex.

11. The Metropolis; the northern peristyle court.

WALL PAINTINGS

The wall paintings of the church are noteworthy for their varied techniques and differing artistic trends. They date from the last decades of the 13th and the first half of the 14th century. On the whole they are not well preserved, and only since the recent cleaning has it been possible to form a clear impression of the artistic quality of the work. Only one relatively large frescoed surface survives in sufficiently good condition to clarify the iconographic arrangement. The wall paintings were probably not executed as a consecutive and organised programme from the beginning. Because the metropolitan church was dedicated to St. Demetrios, the prothesis and the greater part of the northern aisle are occupied by the portrait of the martyr and by scenes from his life and martyrdom; the diaconicon is dedicated to SS. Cosmas and Damian who are pictured full-lenght in the niche, looking towards Christ who is depicted on the quarter-dome. Four scenes depicting their miracles are seen on the walls. Higher up are some dogmatical representations: Christ at the Second Coming and the *Hetoimasia* (Preparation of the Throne). The Virgin Mary is portrayed in the central apse. In a series of panels the cycle of the Feasts, the Passion and the Resurrection are depicted above the colonnade of the central aisle, starting from the sanctuary. The miracles of Jesus, represented partly in the north and partly in the south aisle, occupy an unusually large area. On the vaults and walls of the narthex is the Second Coming, the Councils and other scenes.

The arrangement of scenes and figures of saints in the two aisles is not the same. In the south aisle there is an unusual lack of order, while on the north the walls and arches are covered with pictures in sequence, a fact which proves that the wall paintings were carried out gradually and in sections. We can discern three tendencies, rather than Schools, which differ in their conception of figure, colour and composition.

School A. The decoration of the church seems to have begun in the east part with the work of this School probably between 1270 and 1285. In the apse of the *bema* is the only old painting, the Virgin and Child. Their figures are represented full-length and standing, the type known as "Kyriotissa" or "Nikopoeos". The figure of a cleric, the donor, in prayer, was later erased. To the 14th century belong the Hierarchs on the lower part the paintings on the side walls with Gospel scenes in

12. The Metropolis; narthex, angel from the Last Judgement.

35

13. The Metropolis; the angels from the Majestas Domini *in the diaconicon.*

two rows, and higher up the full-length figures of Four Prophets. The remaining surfaces of the apse are still covered by 17th and 18th century wall paintings.

In the diaconicon, in the second zone, beyond the niche and the miracles of SS. Cosmas and Damian, a *majestas Domini* is depicted in front of the apses with Christ seated between cherubs and adored by eighteen angels. The vault is decorated by the majestic *Hetoimasia* (Preparation of the Throne) with six angels in rhythmic movement executed in a happy synthesis of colours.

The decoration continues in the south vault of the church with the portraits of many saints, five scenes from the life of the Virgin, the Marriage at Cana and Jesus amongst the Doctors.

The Miracles on the same vault belong to School C.

The north wall, beginning from the corresponding apse, displays the following scheme of decoration from bottom to top; a continuous dado, painted in imitation

14. The Metropolis; south apse, the Birth of the Virgin.

15. The Metropolis; south apse, the Marriage at Cana.

16. The Metropolis; south apse, the Virgin and the Priests.

of drapery, then a row of bishops and other military saints, all slightly above life-size. These are followed by a row of martyrs, paired together, half the size of the preceding figures. Above them is a row of medallions containing the busts of saints inscribed on a rectangle decorated in deep blue or red. On the eastern part of the vault are eleven scenes from the Life and Passion of St Demetrius, which reach as far as the prothesis, itself dominated by the representation of the saint placed in the niche. On the western part of the vault the Miracles of Jesus are depicted in two rows: the Healing of the Man with Dropsy and the Healing of the Paralytic on the north side and the Woman of Samaria and the Healing of the Blind Man on the south. On the western tympanum is the Healing of the Lepers.

This "School", represented by artists of varying abilities, is a mixture of various tendencies of the last third of the 13th century. In the lowest row of the north wall the figures stand out quite tranquilly against the dark blue background, with slender bodies and simple linear drapery. The modelling is somewhat more emphasized in the faces, where the pale flesh has delicate green shadows and well drawn features - for example, wrinkles, noses drawn in reddish brown. The second row, with the pairs of martyrs, bears a close resemblance to the characteristics of icon painting: the pose is frontal, the body short, the drapery rec-

17. The Metropolis; north apse, St. Demetrius in prison.

tilinear or curving geometrically. But the faces are distinguished by greater plasticity and a certain portrait-like realism. The busts above them are even more like portable icons, and have lively expressions. In the synaxaries of St.Demetrius or SS. Cosmas and Damian in the diaconicon, executed by a different painter, the composition recalls older menologies. It is simple, widely spaced, and with only elemental buildings and mountains. The colours are few and bright, the conceptions of story-telling simple.The bodies may be tall or short, but their movements are few and stylized. The conservatism of this School seems not to have had a provincial origin as the instructive contemporary murals of St.Euphemia (1280) in Constantinople demonstrate.

School B. A different spirit inspires the figures in the central aisle - the decapitated figures of the scenes from the Life of Christ. The series, which is preserved only above the south colonnade, begins inside the sanctuary: the Annunciation (on the piers of the sanctuary), the Nativity, the Flight into Egypt, the Massacre of the Innocents, the Presentation in the Temple, the Baptism, the Transfiguration, the Raising of Lazarus, the Entry into Jerusalem, the Last Supper and the Betrayal of Judas; on the west wall there are traces of the Crucifixion. No scene is preserved in its entirety. The fragmentary remains, however, allow us to appreciate the

18. The Metropolis; north apse, St. Demetrius preaches in prison.

energetic drive of the new style in its bold search for contrasting colours, its emphasis on plasticity, its crowded compositions, its grace of line and its rhythmic motions which are its chief characteristics. The depiction of the Betrayal is the most daring of the series, with its quick light movements, fluttering drapery, broad free brush strokes and bold colour composition.

Another painter belonging to the same School executed the majestic Last Judgement (or Second Coming) which covers the vaults and the upper part of the walls of the narthex. The rhythmic composition and decorative power needed to transmit the grandeur of such scenes as the Just Judge (damaged) or the better preserved *Hetoimasia* and the enthroned Apostles (on the west wall) did not prevent the artist from using picturesque details in the representation of the Damned, whose punishments contribute to the timely salvation of sinners. The east wall shows the torments of the damned, while the best preserved scenes on the west wall portray the continuation of Hell, where serpents are twined about the evil-faced sinners both male and female. Some have been hanged, others burn in the fires and still others are in Tartarus. Each scene is divided from the others by the fires of Hell which branch out in a decorative way throughout the whole pan-

19. The Metropolis; north apse, the martyrdom of Nestor.
20. The Metropolis; north apse, the martyrdom of St. Demetrius.

21. The Metropolis; north apse, the Healing of the Lepers.

orama. But the grandeur of the composition is centred in the *Hetoimasia,* where the angels are gathered around a majestic throne. Their wings rise, flame-red, in a rhythmical motion of exaltation. Still better preserved are the impetuous Angels with the Book in the arch, to the right and left of the entrance, and the vision of St Peter of Alexandria with the tall figure of the hierarch and the gracious one of Christ. A large inscription in verse above the door refers to the Last Judgement. The Ecumenical Synods are represented on the east wall.

This School, which separates its scenes by means of red bands, is not revolutionary from an iconographic point of view. It is distinguished by vivid motion and action, subject, however, to the rhythmic harmony of the composition. The faces often have a somewhat realistic ugliness, but the figures never lack elegance of pose, grace of line or nobility of expression.

School C. Painters of this school, whose style is related to that of School B, were responsible for the paintings in the western section of the south aisle of the main body of the church. Low down are full-length figures of the twelve Apostles. They are in lively motion, their draperies fluttering, their volume rendered by broad highlights on the material in different combinations of colours e.g. blue highlights on purple material. The broad faces have green shadows on paler flesh, and outlines have an intentional lack of clarity. Above the Apostles, in three zones (one above the windows and two in the vault) and in the western tym-

22. The Metropolis; north apse, Christ and the Woman of Samaria.

panum, the Miracles of Christ in Galilee are represented in an uninterrupted series. Despite the damage they have suffered, recent cleaning has restored one of the most beautiful series of scenes in Mystras. The background is crowded with unrealistic, architectural fantasies in the elegant Hellenistic manner. The scenes are connected with each other by a red curtain which billows out around them, and acts as a stage setting for the episodes taking place in the foreground. There is always a great multitude gathered in groups full of motion, but it always leaves the central slender figure of Christ isolated and peaceful. The whole crowd moves within a given space which is created both by conventional means as well as by the diagonal orientation towards the background of integral parts of the scene, for example buildings or the bed of the Paralytic. This Pompeian arrangement, together with the charm and spaciousness of these representations, recall the decoration of the aristocratic Monastery of Chora (Kariye Djami) in Constantinople.

It seems certain that the more conservative School A, as well as the two others, has close links with Constantinople. This fact lends them an added significance. It is, however, still difficult to express an opinion about the chronological relationship of the Schools. "A" should be the oldest, belonging to the years 1270-1285; "B" and "C", approximately contemporary with each other, cannot be later than the first quarter of the 14th century.

23. *The Metropolis; north apse, the Healing of the Man with Dropsy.*
24. *The Metropolis; north apse, the Healing of the Paralytic.*

25. *The Metropolis; narthex, the Preparation of the Throne.*
26. *The Metropolis; narthex, detail from the Last Judgement.*

THE BRONTOCHION

Near the north corner of the outer wall stand the two largest and most imposing churches of Mystras: those of SS. Theodore and of the Hodegetria, commonly known as the Aphendiko. The foundation of both is linked with one of the most important figures in the newly founded Byzantine state, Pachomios, the energetic archimandrite. He was successively abbot of SS. Theodore and the Monastery of the Hodegetria, and Great Protosyngelos or Ecclesiastical Chancellor of the Peloponnese.

The first mention of SS. Theodore and its founders occurs in a metrical inscription on a fragment of the epistyle of the iconostasis (now in Mystras museum). From this we learn that a certain Daniel, together with Pachomios, built the church. The date must have been about 1290-95, because a manuscript written by a notary Basilakis for the abbot Pachomios in 1296 contains a flattering acrostic which refers to Pachomios as the founder of SS. Theodore. The church is mentioned in an imperial decree, a copy of which is preserved on the wall of the south-west chapel of the Aphendiko, below another of 1322. There is no further mention of the Monastery of SS. Theodore, but the Hodegetria and its founder Pachomios are named in four frescoed decrees of 1313-14, 1318, 1320 and 1322 in the same chapel. These decrees enable us to trace the rapid increase in the property of the "All-Pure Mother of God, the Hodegetria of the church called the Brontochion". This prosperity was due to successive imperial gifts in recognition of the services of the abbot to the central power: "for he has been found well-

27. The Brontochion; in front, SS. Theodore, in the background the Hodegetria.

disposed and sincere towards us". The decrees first recognise and confirm earlier gifts of property to the Monastery, which are to remain tax-free. In addition, they assign to it new districts, farms and villages together with their inhabitants. The Emperors reached the point of ceding to the Monastery "the Latin Quarter" in districts not then actually under their control. From these donations one can begin to understand what a driving force Pachomios must have been, and how therefore he was able to build, within about twenty years, the two most magnificent churches in Mystras.

The earliest mention of the Hodegetria occurs in a manuscript now in Moscow. It was written by Bishop Nikephoros Moschopoulos, and was given by him to the Monastery of the "All-Holy Mother of God of the Brontochion" in 1311-12.

We can therefore conclude that SS. Theodore was begun about 1290 under its abbot Daniel and finished by the abbot Pachomios close to 1296. About 1310 the Hodegetria-Aphendiko was begun by the same Pachomios, who died sometime after 1322.

The relationship between the two neighbouring monastery churches is not clear. The foundation of the one by the abbot and founder of the other within such a short interval of time, and the use by both of the name Brontochion, suggests that the two churches were built originally for the same monastery, and that after the construction of the more impressive Hodegetria, the monastery changed its name. This hypothesis is strengthened by the fact that around SS. Theodore, on the surface at least, there are no traces of monastic buildings such as the refectory or cells, whereas at the Aphendiko many of these still stand to a considerable height. On the other hand, excavations around SS. Theodore revealed a series of graves on both the north and the south sides, sufficient to characterise it as a cemetery, as the Evangelistria was in later times. It is possible, therefore, that when the Hodegetria was built as the catholicon of the Monastery, SS. Theodore was designated as the cemetery church for the monks.

The church of SS. Theodore, which is one of the oldest in Mystras, belongs to the type called greek-cross domed octagon because the great dome is supported not on four arches which form a square as in the usual type of cross-in-square church, but on eight arches which describe an octagon. Four of the eight arches are prolonged into vaults which form a cross, while the other four, at the corners, deepen into squinches. In this system, the weight of the great dome is distributed before being transmitted to the walls. This type of construction probably originated in Constantinople, but in the 11th century we meet it fully developed in the area of Hellas at Hosios Loukas in Beotia, Soteira Lykodemou (the Russian church) in Athens, Daphni, St. Nicholas in the Fields near Skripou and Cristianou. In the 13th century we find it again in St. Sophia at Monemvasia as a simplified copy of Daphni. It is probably from Monemvasia that the type was copied in Mystras.

At SS. Theodore, the octagonal church takes on all the characteristics of the "Greek School" of architecture. The women's gallery has been abolished, barrel vaults replaced groin vaults throughout, and there is no narthex. Finally, the supports of the dome are solid walls, except on the west where two marble columns made greater aesthetic impact. The main characteristic of the type remains: the enormous dome with the high drum dominating the whole width of the church. It creates a large, high central space to which the arms of the cross are complementary. The unified effect provided by the central space is enhanced by the separate treatment of the four small chambers formed between the arms of the cross.

28. SS. Theodore, east side.

Those on the west do not open at all; the others open only indirectly into the church proper, and do not interfere with the harmonious curves of the central area.

The uninterrupted interior surfaces of the walls are covered by warm-toned frescoes which continue up to the top of the arch, in contrast to the treatment at Daphni where a carved moulding at the spring of the arches adds plasticity to the surface. The unity of the enclosed space and its relatively restricted dimension effectively create a peculiarly intimate atmosphere. In this feeling of intimacy the church of SS. Theodore stands apart from the other monuments of its type, which more often reflect a search for impressive and monumental grandeur.

On the exterior, some difficulty was experienced in satisfactorily connecting the cubic mass of the building with the relatively enormous dome, which consists of a high drum with sixteen narrow windows and a large cupola. This difficulty was overcome here in a way not employed elsewhere. Here, the eastern facade, with

49

its low shallow three-sided apses is divided, from the base of the window upwards, by saw-tooth courses cutting off five wide horizontal zones, three with *cloisonné masonry* and two which must have had a veneer of glazed plaques not now preserved. This alternation of plain and polychrome zones emphasized the horizontal lines of the building. The transition from the body of the church to the high dome was effected by the roofs, which mount step by step to a pyramid high above the sanctuary and leave the side arms of the cross free-standing. Note that the middle window of the apse is higher than the flanking blind windows, which in turn are higher than the windows of the lateral apses; thus the crowns of the windows, descending towards the edges, follow a line analogous to the slope of the roofs.

A similar method was employed on the west facade, now obscured by a slightly later narthex, probably added under the influence of the style of the Aphendiko, and with the same two-storeyed tower-like chapels at the ends. Five arched doorways, the middle one higher than the others, bestow a monumental character on the facade, even though the lack of absolute symmetry (the two southern doorways are the same height, the two to the north are unequal) shows that this was not a primary concern in that period. The facade is crowned by a gable of the western arm of the cross, pierced by a two-lobed window, which had two courses of *cloisonné masonry* and a corresponding course of veneer. Here too the saw-tooth courses are the dominant decorative element; they surround the windows, separate the different zones, run around the arches of the doorways and give a feeling of life and animation to the whole facade. The gables of the side arms of the cross are each adorned by a two-lobed window with two flanking half-arches; the whole surface has linear ornament of brickwork, although the upper part is modern reconstruction. Decorative glazed plates were let into the gables of all three arms of the cross.

Thus the latest known example of the "octagonal" type of church is distinguished by contrasts, by variety in combining masses and planes in the decoration and by use of the interior space to create an intimate impression rather than a monumental one. Nevertheless, SS. Theodore had no successors. The splendid Aphendiko, built only a few years later, was the "modern" building of the time, and had greater influence on the later churches of Mystras.

WALL PAINTINGS

Only a few fragments of the mural decoration have been preserved and they are in bad condition. There is, however, enough to reconstruct approximately the iconographic arrangement.

An imitation of marble veneer was painted from floor level to the height of about one metre. Above that, as in the Metropolis, a row of full-length warrior saints stands rather larger than life size. Remains of a few have been preserved; they stand in a frontal position, though not very firmly, on their tiny feet. The figures are hard, without much feeling. Details are few, and the execution is somehow impressionistic and hasty. The colours of the clothing tend to warm reds and browns, with broad blue highlights picking out the folds. The shading on the faces is green or greenish. The freedom of execution and vitality which characterizes the figures, together with the colour combinations, suggest that these frescoes are imitations of School A in the Metropolis.

A second band of frescoes depicting small scenes lies above the saints. It included the piers of the sanctuary on which the Annunciation was depicted and the flat surfaces of the arms of the cross. On the south side are slight traces of scenes from the Life of the Virgin (the Nativity, the Entrance to the Temple). The third and highest band, which fills the vaults of the cross, would have contained the Twelve Feasts and scenes from the Gospels. In the west arm there are traces of the Denial of Peter on the south wall; of the Lament at the Tomb on the tympanum; of the Women at the Tomb on the north wall, and, on the vault of the north arm, of the Pentecost. It is difficult to distinguish the style of these frescoes, but they seem to be related to that of the saints in the lowest row.

In the south-east chapel more has been preserved but it is in bad condition. The chapel was almost certainly dedicated to the Virgin, probably as the Zoodochos Pigi, as the appropriate scene in the apse suggests. On the south wall, the SS. Theodore are shown interceding with the enthroned Virgin; beside them stand an angel and a priest, on behalf of a suppliant whose broad-brimmed conical hat is barely distinguishable. On the north wall, between the large figure of an angel and an equally imposing John the Baptist stands a small Emperor or Despot, wearing an embroidered tunic and yellow conical headdress. The vault was decorated with scenes from the Life of the Virgin; on the north side and fairly well preserved, is the Birth of the Virgin with graceful figures, tall and slender, and, in the background, stylized architectural elements. The colours are dark, with shadows and highlights of different tones in the same colour. The Presentation of the Virgin and the Nativity occupy the south wall. On the tympanum of the west wall is the Dormition of the Virgin, with the episode of the Hebrew Jephonia in front. These frescoes are to be dated around 1400.

The north-east chapel has a tomb on the north side; and on the opposite wall which blocks communication with the prothesis is a representation of a Manuel Palaiologos, identified by an inscription written in capital letters. He wears a robe of deep blue, and has passed his handkerchief through his yellow belt. He kneels in front of the Virgin who stands veiled in red and holding the Child. Low down, in small hastily written letters of another hand, is the date of his death, which may be read as 1423. The suppliant is usually identified with Manuel II Palaiologos. Against this identification must be set the fact that Manuel died in 1425, and was not buried in Mystras. Moreover, this figure is wearing simple civilian dress, and the ungrammatical, mis-spelled inscription makes no mention of imperial identity.

SCULPTURED DECORATION

The similarity and the mediocre quality of the few surviving pieces of sculpture show that they belong to the same period as the church, and were presumably made especially for this building. Proof of this is provided by the single fragment of the epistyle of the iconostasis now in the Museum on which is incised the dedicatory inscription referring to the founders Daniel and Pachomios: its decoration in nearly flat relief is crowded, reminiscent of Islamic motifs, and the technique, far from flawless, may be compared with with that of some shrines in the Museum. The base of the drum of the dome is accented by a stone cornice, semi-circular in section, and carved with a stylized rinceau so intertwined as to leave elliptical spaces which are filled with bunches of grapes. These are examples of the local sculpture of Mystras at the end of the 13th century.

HODEGETRIA-APHENDIKO

The building was preserved fairly well until the 19th century. About 1863 most of the columns were removed, resulting in the collapse of the dome and part of the vaults. In 1938, the Department of Restoration under the supervision of Professor Orlandos began the careful and tasteful restoration of the colonnade of the ground floor, the roof of the side aisles, the vaults, the three-lobed window of the apse of the sanctuary and the dome. All the work was based on evidence from the building itself. The reconstruction of the bell-tower also repays study.

ARCHITECTURE

The catholicon of the Monastery which Pachomios erected in the name of the Hodegetria has an entirely different character from the church of SS. Theodore, despite the fact that the two monuments are separated by only twenty years. The Aphendiko declares very plainly the intention to create a large and impressive building which would recall the capital of the Empire.

Externally, the building looks like a two storey five domed cross-in-square church; internally, however, it exhibits a peculiarity. The ground floor is a basilica divided into three aisles by two rows of three columns, while on the upper storey the complete system of a four-column cross-in-square church with five domes has been superimposed. This system is supported by the two colonnades of the basilicas, and by the outer walls which are lightly buttressed on both facades in a vertical line corresponding to the lateral arches. Thus, in the side aisles, the arches which unite the columns with the outer walls, divide each side aisle into five parts which are roofed with saucer domes. This solid ceiling permits the existence of an upper gallery exactly above, and this continues round to cover the prothesis and the diaconicon, as in Hellenistic basilica. The west side of the gallery is above the narthex, which is thus incorporated organically in the church. The ceiling of the gallery consists of a high dome over the narthex, while over the side aisles are the great barrel vaults of the north and south arms of the cross, together with the four smaller domes at the corners. These smaller domes counteract the lateral thrust of the vaults, which thereby receive the load of the vast central dome.

This composite form of basilica and cross-in-square church is rather rare out-side Mystras, and its history has not yet been written. The domed basilica is a common type in the Byzantine era, but its originality here lies in the fact that it is not a simple dome set over the colonnade, but the complete system of a Constantinopolitan five-domed cross-in-square, resting not on the ground, but on the basilica beneath. It is reminiscent of older churches such as St. Irene, but only in

29. View of the Hodegetria from the north; the two side chapels in the fore-ground.

30. The Hodegetria from the north-west. ▶

the large chapel of St. Nicholas of Katapoliani on Paros, contemporary with the large 6th century church, as in Hagia Sophia at Vizyi (east Thrace) of the 8th century is the same type used. However, types and traditions are so successfully combined here that nothing seems experimental, and one is only conscious of the excellence of the unusual scheme.

As we enter the church by the north door from the low narthex, the luminous height of the central area, enclosed by the interlocking curves of vaults, arches and dome, creats an immediate impression. The contrast provided by the side aisles with their low ceilings and subdued half-light, still further emphasizes the character of the central space which seems to rise above us in a song of praise.

Externally, the Aphendiko appears to be a complex of various buildings. At either end of the narthex are two-storeyed chapels built like towers. Both the north and the west sides of the church are colonnaded. At the southern end of the west colonnade stands the three-storey bell-tower, finely proportioned and built in *cloisonné masonry*; the northern colonnade is constricted by two additional chapels. The masonry of the church itself differs from the other churches of Mystras, for the Greek *cloisonné* system has been abandoned in favour of ordinary cut stone with narrow horizontal rows of brick. At the east end, the massive semi-circular central apse is pierced by three-lobed windows below and by two rows of blind arcades above, and the two side apses are decorated in the same way. These false windows, of the type found elsewhere only in the buildings of Constantinople and Salonica, emphasize the plastic quality of the apse.

The colonnades which so gracefully decorate the facades of the churches of Mystras have their origins in Constantinople, where this ancient Greek motif always continued in use. They are, however, adapted with such skill to the demands of the site that they seem inseparable from it. The colonnades, which were an innovation for the Greek school of Byzantine architecture, were introduced into the capital of the Despotat with the construction of the Aphendiko. On the north and west sides, the arcaded colonnades were roofed with saucer domes.

The south colonnade has been preserved, but it suffered from re-modelling in the 14th century, so that in its present form it consists of a funerary chapel with *arcosolia* and tombs round about. It was originally two-storeyed. The lower storey had four large arched openings, and the upper had three three-lobed windows placed unsymmetrically in relation to the openings below. Of these windows, the central one was probably crowned with a double concentric arch; those at the sides with a pair of blind arches (the same theme as at the eastern end) and with a great deal of decorative brickwork. It seems that in 1366, when the abbot Kyprianos added the tasteless chapel to the eastern end of the arcade, the floor dividing the two storeys was still in existence. Later builders closed the lower arches to make *arcosolia,* removed the intervening floor, blocked up the door leading from the eastern chapel to the upper storey and adorned the wall with frescoes.

Thus the catholicon of the Hodegetria of the Brontochion, built immediately after the rather conservative and locally designed buildings of the Metropolis and SS. Theodore, brings elements of the architectural style of Constantinople to the provincial capital. The Hodegetria influenced later buildings, such as St. Sophia, and more especially the Pantanassa, and it inspired the re-modelling of others, such as the work of Matthew at the Metropolis. It also gave many elements to other local types of church, such as the exterior colonnade and bell-tower, all of which combine at Mystras to create a special architectural style.

31. The Hodegetria; the restored roof and domes.

SCULPTURED DECORATION

Luxurious decoration was rarely indulged in even in the capital, and Pachomios' effort to make his church unusually elegant is shown by the use of marble revetments on all the interior walls of the lower floor. This marble veneer was combined with wall paintings. In the narthex and in the main church arched frames surrounded the standing saints (neither the frames nor the saints are preserved today), and in the sanctuary there was a double row of framed church Fathers. The arches of the frames, as well as of the aisles, were inlaid with small multi-coloured plaques. Only three of these are preserved, all in the eastern arch of the south colonnade, coloured black, white and violet.

The marble revetment was crowned by a frieze of ornament in flat relief (a fragment of which is preserved in the apse of the diaconicon), and a cornice of painted decoration imitating the carved theme of the door jambs: in the centre is a cross from which springs a wavy branch with leaves. The same theme is found again in the crowning moulding of the only surviving original capital - the eastern one of the southern row of columns. Above the arches the angular cornice is decorated with a row of deeply caved *anthemia*, probably contemporary with the church. This angular cornice runs round the middle apse of the sanctuary; there, below the cornice on a fragment of a marble string course, are a few of the carved letters of the inscription "Great is the glory of this house; the last shall be first saith the Lord".

WALL PAINTINGS

The polychrome marble decoration was supplemented by frescoes. The variety of spaces provided by the architectural scheme made it easy to establish several separate iconographic units which followed the horizontal division between basilica and cross-in-square church.

On the lower floor, as we have seen, there was a standing saint on every section of the marble revetment. In the tympana, under the arch, were pairs of martyrs, nearly all of which are well preserved.

In the arches and the saucer domes were the figures of the more important saints such as St. Antony and St. Andrew. Cherubims occupied the pendentives of the saucer domes. The series continues in the sanctuary in the same manner, except that in the apses of the prothesis and the diaconicon the Hierarchs stood in continuous arched frames, no longer preserved.

In the central apse the Hierarchs are in a double row, ten above and six below: Gregory of Nyssa, Sylvester, Basil, Gregory the Theologian, Clement, Gregory of Armenia, Pope Leo of Rome and others, all turning towards the centre of the apse. Above the Hierarchs is the Communion of the Apostles, and themes relating to the Eucharist. The Virgin enthroned between two angels occupies the quarter dome of the apse, and the Ascension the vault which covers the sanctuary. Below the Ascension, on the north wall, is the Doubting of Thomas, and on the south the Appearance of Jesus to the Eleven.

In the gallery the Gospel cycle unfolds on the curving soffits of the arches, readily visible to the congregation below. The cycle begins on the south wall of the sanctuary with the Nativity, and continues opposite with the Presentation. The Baptism and Transfiguration are on the south arch. The other Feasts would have been on the west and north together with the Raising of Lazarus, the Entry into Jerusalem and episodes of the Passion and Resurrection. The only one to have been preserved is the scene of the Holy Women at the Sepulchre, which is on the north tympanum. On the flat wall surfaces of the gallery are more arched frames, filled with pairs of standing saints. These are the Seventy Apostles. In the four small domes and in the saucer domes are Biblical Patriarchs and Prophets, surrounded by Cherubim and Seraphim. This arrangement of cycles and scenes presents nothing unusual for the period. The iconography of the sanctuary, where the Ascension is linked with the Doubting of Thomas and the Appearance to the

32. The Hodegetria; the western dome of the gynaikonitis, the Virgin and Prophets.

59

33. The Hodegetria; narthex, from the Miracles of Jesus.

Eleven, corresponds to the excerpts from the Gospels which are read on the two sundays after Easter, the feast of St. Thomas and at Ascensiontide.

Each fresco reflects the characteristics of painting of the period. In the depiction of the Nativity many scenes have been co-ordinated into one composition. The central figure is the Virgin, who reclines with graceful dignity and tenderness beside the manger; at the left the Magi are arriving on horseback while a group of angels descends from above. Below, to the left, an angel leads two women to wash the Child; one of them is the mid-wife Salome. To the right, another angel leads the Magi with their gifts. The shepherds are depicted on the lower right. All these figures are very small and scattered, with little cohesion between them, so that their significance is simply complementary to the dominating central figure of the Virgin. In the scene of the Baptism, the figures of the Baptist and the Angels are bigger than the tiny form of Christ, and the scene is filled out with children in lively motion and picturesque attitudes, with personifications of the Jordan and the sea, and fishnets.

In the apse of the sanctuary the Communion of the Apostles forms a band crowded with figures, although it is a rhythmic composition with many imaginative details. Although the Apostles are shown in elegant attitudes, they have been painted with life-like ugliness. In the depiction of the Ascension the Apostles

34. The Hodegetria; narthex the raising of Peter's wife's mother and the Healing of the Blind Man.

are packed together, gesturing animatedly like men in a market place. Near each group an angel addresses the Apostles with serene grace. The Virgin is a striking contrast; she stands calmly in a hieratic frontal pose. Above all is the majestic figure of Christ, surrounded by a mandorla held by four angels. The entire composition derives its dramatic character from the contrasts of movement and passivity.

The characteristic feature of all these paintings is the emphatic and repeated broad brush strokes with which the colour has been laid on. In the Baptism, the landscape is light green with pale brown shadows and occasional tones of a purplish-brown; the entire luminous composition is painted in these simple colours. Similarly, in the scene of the Holy Women at the Sepulchre, the colours are few and glowing. The deep red cave is set off by the green mountain; the angel wears a green chiton and a brownish-red himation with broad white highlights; in the figures of the women the combinations are dark brown with light blue, or light yellow with green. This impressionistic method of putting complementary colours side by side to give the effect of lively modelling is still better seen in the figures of the Seventy Apostles in the gallery. Their firm stance, their aristocratic expressions and the classic folds of their clothing all suggest an inspiration derived from ancient statues. The painting has been executed in contrasting colours; yellow

35. The Hodegetria; gynaikonitis, *the Just Zacharias.*

with green, red with light green, broad white highlights and light blue backgrounds. The Old Testament Patriarchs and the Cherubim on the ceiling of the north gallery were painted with still freer brush strokes. Abraham's hair and beard cascade in torrents, in light blue flecked with white and brown. The wings of the Cherubim are yellow and are tipped with sparkling feathers of flaming red. That this kind of harmony of colours was of major interest to the painters appears from the fact that the colour combinations noted are sometimes found on the same garment, sometimes on two separate garments of the same person and sometimes on two figures seated side by side. In the frescoes we have described, at least three different modes of modelling and colour combination can be distinguished, but this does not necessarily imply the work of a different artist.

In the northern section of the narthex, above the lost revetment, are the Miracles of Christ: the Healing of the Blind Man, the Raising of Peter's wife's mother, the Healing of the Man with Dropsy, the Women of Samaria and the Marriage at Cana. On the south tympanum is the scene of Christ amongst the Elders. Other scenes have recently been cleaned. Above the entrance to the church is the Zoodochos Pigi, in which the Virgin is represented in the Blacherniotissa type, with Joachim praying on her right and Anna on her left; above are two small angels.

The Miracles on the ground floor of the narthex, the scenes of the Passion, the

36-37. The Hodegetria; a holy monk — St Gregory of Armenia.

38. The Hodegetria; north-west chapel, the martyrs, detail from All Saints.

Virgin with the Prophets and the saints in the west gallery were all painted by an artist of another School which was responsible also for the north chapel of the narthex. This School is characterized by the very restrained use of motion which reaches the point of absolute stillness so that the figures seem to unfold as if in a frieze, all in one plane. The slender silhouettes, whether in slow rhythmic motion or in graceful poses, bring us close to certain mosaics of the Monastery of Chora (Karije Djami); the beautiful face of the Virgin, above the entrance, is still closer to the Deesis of the same church.

39-40. The Hodegetria; south-west chapel, detail from the vaulted ceiling, angels-Karyatids holding the mandorla of Christ.

The Chapels

In the north chapel of the narthex are two tombs. That of the abbot Pachomios stands near the west wall. In the *arcosolium* there are still traces of the frescoes which show the kneeling Pachomios offering the church to the standing Virgin. Angels bearing torches are crowed together in the cornice of the *arcosolium,* and the scene resembles the Communion of the Apostles in the sanctuary apse.

Against the north wall stands the tomb of the Despot Theodore II Palaiologos, who died in 1443 as a Theodoritos monk. He is represented twice in the *arcosolium,* to the left in the resplendent dress of the Despot, and to the right in the simple habit of a monk. The latter is better preserved.

The walls of this funerary chapel, which occupies both storeys, are divided into three zones, and on each side is painted a choir of Prophets, Apostles, Patriarchs and Martyrs and Ascetics. All walk from right to left, their gaze cast upwards to the Pantocrator in the dome, which, together with the Virgin and St. John the Baptist in attitudes of supplication on the south tympanum, forms a Deesis. The meaning of this scheme of decoration is explained by a scene on the east wall, where, in a high niche, Christ enthroned in glory is represented as the Just Judge. Part of an inscription is preserved around the arch of the niche; it begs the intercession of the Virgin, the Baptist and all the saints for mercy and the salvation of the souls of all those buried in the chapel.

One of the best works of the school of painters which decorated the narthex is the panel of Martyrs on the west wall of the chapel. The painter employed broad surfaces of colours: all were pale shades, almond green, light blue and wine reds, and these soft colours were used interchangeably on garments and their borders, for the sky and the ground. They were used in many tones and shades, and the general effect has a velvety quality. The modelling in the faces is broad and round; the flesh tones are light pink with light shadows of green, and delicate white highlights intensify the modelling. This School exhibits an intentional archaism by representing slim feet barely touching the ground, and sparse folds which fall almost straight as in early mosaics. Such mosaics, for example those of Ravenna, are also recalled by the jewelled borders on the robes of the martyrs. Moreover, the human figures are idealized and unrealistic; nevertheless, the small eyes, set close together, resemble faces painted by the Italian artist Cavallini (1250-1338), and, even more, the mosaics of the Kilisse-Djami at Constantinople. The group of the Apostles, St. Paul and the Deesis of the dome are painted in the same style. The other groups belong rather to the dominant trend in the murals of the church.

The south-west chapel of the narthex is poorly lit. All four walls are covered from top to bottom with copies of imperial decrees (chrysobulls) issued by various emperors on behalf of the Monastery of the Hodegetria of Brontochion. On the vaulted ceiling, four flying angels hold in their upraised hands the circular mandorla surrounding the figure of Christ, no longer preserved. Four groups of rays radiate from the mandorla, each reaching to a hand, and each hand holds an unrolled decree. Thus the rights of the Monastery are protected with this symbolic scene which attributes Imperial favours to God. The oldest decree is that furthest to the east (to the left as one enters), and dates to 1312-13. The latest is dated to 1322; it is above the entrance and covers an earlier one. Below the wings of the angels are four iambic verses of three lines each which record the untiring efforts of Pachomios for the good of the Monastery.

The themes described so far belong to a common composition, which is painted in an impressionistic manner. From the corners and out of the foliage spring poles, possibly columns, decorated with garlands which curve over to form four arches as in a festive pavilion. Above it fly the four angels which are amongst the finest figures of the Aphendiko. They display more grace than the corresponding delicate figures of the Ascension in the sanctuary, although they belong to the same School, and they are more precise in form and proportion and show greater rhythm in their wheeling motion. Finally the manner in which the circular space is filled is unusually impressive.

This particular composition is important also for the general chronology of the frescoes. It must be agreed that Pachomios had decorated the chapel before the final decree was issued in 1322, since underneath it are the traces of an older decree referring to the SS. Theodore. In any case, the decoration was not carried out before 1312-13 when the first decree was issued.

In the small south-east chapel the wall paintings on the east side represent the Last Supper, and John Euchaites before the three enthroned Hierarchs. This is the story of the vision that solved the question of the standing of the three bishops, Basil, Gregory and John Chrysostom. On the west side are symbolic representations of the teachings of the three bishops. The execution is hasty and somewhat careless, but it retains a rhythmic elegance in the postures and outlines. The date of the decoration is fixed by the monogram of the abbot Kyprianos, of 1366, which is above the entrance to the chapel.

No frescoes have been preserved in the four *arcosolia* of the south portico, originally a colonnade and later the burial place of the nobles. In the arcosolium to the west is a representation of a nobleman wearing a rich garment of red, patterned in yellow in imitation of brocade. His handkerchief is drawn through his belt. The head has been destroyed. In the centre of the composition stood the Virgin and Child, and on the other side was the wife of the nobleman, wearing an equally elegant red garment. It was once possible to decipher the name Kariotis.

On the walls over the arches are successive scenes from the Death and Burial of the Virgin, following the apocryphal text. The central saucer dome is occupied by the Slaughter of the Innocents, and the two groin vaults by the history of Zacharias and of the Nativity. The style here is quite different from any other in the church. The crowd moves intimately within a defined space among furniture and buildings, sometimes realistic, sometimes fanciful. The colour scheme (clear after the recent cleaning) shows harmonic contrasts of bright tones of soft blue, green, ochre and warm chestnut brown. Many hands are discernible, but the drawing, hasty and careless, recalls the "far Presto" style. This tendency is found over a wide area, from Bulgaria (Ivanovo) to Russia (Volotovo).

41. St. Sophia seen from the east.

ST. SOPHIA

On the south-west side of the hill, in the district of the Palace, but rather higher than the square, stands St. Sophia, the Palace church and the catholicon of a small monastery. Manuel Katakouzenos, the first Despot of the Morea (1348-1380), left monograms on the capitals of the pilasters which read "Manuel Katakouzenos, Palaiologos, Despot, Ktetor". A long poem, copied by Fourmont, the early French antiquary from the original inscription on the colonnade of the church, tells us that portraits of Manuel's parents were once in front of the entrance. The original has not survived.

This church, dedicated to the Word of the Father, was identified by me many years ago with the church of Christ Zoodotes (the Giver of Life), which was founded by Manuel. A partiarchal decree of 1365 permitted its transformation into the catholicon of a monastery, so that it is possible to date the building to the years 1351 -1365.

The monastery of the Zoodotes was the burial place of at least two royal consorts in the 15th century; Theodora Tokkou, wife of Constantine Palaiologos, was interred here after 1429, and Kleopa Malatesta, wife of the Despot Theodore, about 1433 (see section on the Pantanassa). Three square domed chambers on the west and south of the bell-tower which still preserve fragments of wall paintings and *opus sectile* in the pavement may be considered to be the royal tombs.

Until the year 1938 the church was in a poor state of preservation, but thanks to Professor Orlandos' careful restoration the dome and the northern colonnade have been re-built, the windows of the apse unblocked, the debris cleared away and in the interior a pillar, which had been substituted for one of the columns, has been replaced by a new column.

ARCHITECTURE

The church belongs to the same type as the Peribleptos and the Evangelistria, that is to the simple two-column type of the cross-in-square church. Its dome rests on two columns to the west, and at the east on the two walls which separate the parts of the sanctuary. Thus the vault of the eastern arm of the cross covers the sanctuary. This plan distinguishes the simple type, which is the most common in Greece, from the so-called complex type of Constantinople, exemplified in Mystras by the upper storey of the Aphendiko. In the complex type the dome is supported by four columns, and the eastern arm of the cross does not include the sanctuary.

St. Sophia is distinguished also by its tall narrow proportions which emphasize its height, a feature unusual in Byzantine architecture. The church is lit only from a few narrow windows in the dome, and from those in the arms of the cross, all high up. On the outside, the tendency towards height is less emphasized. The only side free of colonnades, the eastern, has three shallow narrow three-sided apses which rise without any decoration other than the carefully laid *cloisonné masonry*.

St. Sophia, alone of its type, has a spacious narthex with a dome, the height of which does not exceed that of the western arm of the cross. On the exterior are two elegant colonnades. That on the north side, with a view towards the valley of the Eurotas, has been re-built, while the other, on the west, which overlooks a court with chapels, is now in ruins. At the west end of the northern colonnade is the neat bell-tower. It was originally a three-storeyed building, but only two storeys now remain, together with parts of the inner stairway. During the Turkish Occupation the building served as a minaret while the church was turned into a mosque.

A spacious chapel projects from the eastern end of the northern colonnade. Its construction is similar to that of the apses, so that it is probably contemporary with the church.

The external decoration of the church is simple, but carefully executed. Those wall surfaces which are not covered by colonnades or chapels are executed in fine *cloisonné masonry* with a row of brick saw-tooth below the roof. The gables of the arms of the cross are richly decorated with brickwork, and their two-lobed windows are emphasized by the double row of bricks and the large saw-tooth arch which surrounds them. The windows of the apses have less elaborate decoration.

Internally, exceptional attention was paid to the pavement of many-coloured marble which surround marble inlays of geometric design.

The plain *cloisonné* surfaces, clean rectangular outlines and strongly marked surface keep the building's main characteristics true to the Greek tradition, in both type and construction. As a decorative feature providing colour and variety, the ornamental brickwork is emphasized here more than in the earlier churches, but nevertheless it remains a secondary characteristic.

Various other elements have been added to this Greek core. The architecture of St. Sophia was influenced by the size and splendour of the Aphendiko. From the Aphendiko were derived the domed narthex, the two picturesque colonnades with their curving lines, and the bell-tower, although its connection there with the main building is loose. Moreover, the architect of St. Sophia included the north-east chapel in his original plan in imitation of the Aphendiko, although there the south-east chapel was a later addition. The light, narrow proportions, especially in the disposition of the interior spaces, can be attributed to western influence.

SCULPTURED DECORATION

The sculptured decoration of the church, in so far as it has been preserved, is meagre. The capital of a single column and the epistyle of the pseudo-pilasters are decorated with a row of *anthemia* separated by a triple leaf. In the middle of each side, in the place of the *anthemia,* is either the monogram referred to above or a double-headed eagle. The execution is mediocre and somewhat provincial. Two fragments of the epistyle of the iconostasis are of interest; one is still in place, the other is in the museum. Both bear representations of animals — a lion on one and a griffin on the other — clutching their prey, and executed in relief on a ground of delicately worked branches. At the end of each piece, on a lower plane, is a branch in relief, far inferior in skill and technique to the rest of the work and comparable to the *anthemia*. These are probably fragments of the 12th century, re-used and supplemented with new carving on the worn surfaces.

WALL PAINTINGS

The fresco decoration of the church is visible in only a few places, but from the little that remains it is possible to reconstruct an iconographic arrangement comparable to that of the Peribleptos.

70

42. St. Sophia; Christ in the apse of the sanctuary (detail).

In the sanctuary is a large enthroned Christ, traces of the Eucharistic scenes and Hierarchs. In the vault is the Ascension. Around the lower part of the walls a dado, 1.50 m. high, imitates marble revetment, as in the Peribleptos. The major Feasts are depicted in the three high vaults of the cross, the Passion in the two low western vaults.

The decoration of the north-east chapel is now in poor condition. Christ, surrounded by Angels, Principalities and Powers, can be distinguished in the vault. Two large full-length Archangels, stress the funerary character of the chapel which also contains a 15th century tomb. The Annunciation on the east, the Crucifixion on the west, the Dormition of the Virgin on the south, the Descent to Hell on the north and the Man of Sorrows in the little niche may be seen.

In the relatively large dome of the south-east chapel the figure of the Virgin Mary, Blacherniotissa, may be picked out. As in the Peribleptos, she is surrounded by the Divine Liturgy. On the west wall is the Birth of the Virgin, an intimate scene with picturesque details and traditional garments. On the north wall there is a full-length figure of the enthroned Christ.

It is impossible to speak of the technical and aesthetic quality of the frescoes in their present state of preservation.

The poem referred to at the beginning of the section suggests that the two outer galleries, the north and west, were decorated with frescoes. Traces of paintings remain in the chapels connected with the bell-tower, and in the chapel which lies at the south-west corner of the west court, where only the vault of the apse still stands. Fragments of an attractive imitation of drapery and marble are preserved in the two-storeyed refectory of the monastery which lies north-west of the church. Heads of saints are still visible in some of the niches.

Further west stand various small buildings for the daily use of the monastery, beyond a fine cistern which has remained undamaged.

43. *The Peribleptos; the sanctuary with the chapels.*

THE PERIBLEPTOS

The little monastery of the Peribleptos was built near the south-east corner of the outer wall directly against the precipitous rock. There are no documentary sources for the history of the monastery, and the information to be derived from the church itself is scant.

No name has been preserved on the painted representation of the founders, although it is clear that they were a noble couple. A double monogram is preserved above the door of the later side narthex: it reads "of Leo Mavropapas". Mavropapas was a well-known family. Finally, above the arched doorway, is a plaque decorated in relief with two heraldic lions rampant, the round monogram of the Peribleptos in the middle and a row of lilies. A later restorer added "5 March 1714. Built at the expense of Panayiotis Thebaios", that is, in the brief period when the Venetians held Mystras. The lion rampant occurs again; once on a decorative plaque built into the wall near the southern two-lobe window, once on a plaque bearing the monogram of the Katakouzenoi, now in the Museum at the Metropolis. The Lusignans, however, had the same emblem. The lily also occurs again, in the carved decoration found both inside and outside the apse. All these must be emblems belonging to the noble family which built the monastery, emblems with strong Frankish influence. In this connection it is worth remembering that the wife of the Despot Manuel Katakouzenos was Isabella de Lusignan, and that the donors portrayed in the church have not yet been identified.

The position of the church beside, and partly under, the rocky hillside, led earlier investigators such as Curtius and Ross to identify the site with the "Eleusinian sanctuary" mentioned by Pausanias. This hypothesis has been rejected by more recent scholars. The somewhat strange location of the church is explained by the suggestion that an early Christian place of worship had existed in the cave west of the church, now the chapel of St. Katherine, and that the Peribleptos was built in the 14th century to beautify and enlarge the earlier shrine.

Two of the monastery buildings have been preserved; the church with its annexes, and high, tower-like building which has been called the refectory. On its upper sections it exhibits the same Frankish characteristics as the bell-tower of the Pantanassa.

ARCHITECTURE

The plan of the church is not rectangular because it was compelled to follow the lines of the hollow of the rock into which the church was built. Comparable peculiarities are found in the Metropolis where the contours of the hill also obliged the architects to adapt their plan. In the Peribleptos the rock precludes the existence of an entrance in the middle of the west side, and in its place is a niche. On the same side a door leads into the chapel of St. Katherine, set under the rock with the apse of its sanctuary on the south side. Outside, below the apses of the church, two connecting chapels were built, one with a small dome. The apses of these chapels project over the rock edge like balconies. Since there is no place for a direct entrance to the church a small door beside the apses leads to a low narrow corridor in the rock, whence one suddenly finds oneself inside the church, beneath the north arm of the cross.

The Peribleptos belongs to the so-called simple two-colum type of church (cf. St. Sophia). The lengthening of the western arm of the cross should be noted as a special feature. It is made possible by the existence of barrel vaults which cover the side aisles, a Greek characteristic, since in the corresponding place in Constantinopolitan examples, groin vaults, demanding strict symmetry, were built. In the Peribleptos the remarkable elongation of the western part, and the resulting disproportionately big arches, disturbs the uniform rhythm in the upward movement of the space; in the smaller St. Sophia the proportions are more harmonious.

The apses of the church are five sided. The central one, and the prothesis, have a window, the diaconicon apse has only a small interior niche. The polygonal shape of the apses is not particularly Greek, but the spirit of the land is reflected in their simple decoration. This consists of a lower zone with two rosettes with a floral motif between them, and an upper zone with a double row of brick saw-tooth underlining the crowning tiles. Peculiar to the Peribleptos is the stone moulding between the two rows of saw-tooth. It has a wide channel in the middle, bordered by delicate guilloche on its upper edge. It is interesting to note that the moulding with the guilloche appears to be the continuation of a carved marble fragment with a rinceau perhaps of 12th century date, built into the central apse. The guilloche pattern in also found in the interior, around the base of the dome. In 1714, Panayiotis Thebaios decorated his monumental gate in a similar style. Outside, the apses are built in the usual Greek *cloisonné* style, very carefully executed. The work, however, is confined to those parts of the building which can be seen, namely the apses, the east and south arms of the cross and the drum (tympanum) of the dome.

The rest of the exterior decoration is simple. On the gables of the arms of the cross a row of reliefs framed by saw-tooth work, were built into the wall; only one of these has survived. Plates were set into the eastern gable. Two false half-arches were built around the two-lobed window of the south gable. Each of the windows in the light and graceful dome is framed by a double arch within a third arched row of saw-tooth.

Originally, there was a porch on the south side of the building. It was later remodelled, perhaps by Leo Mavropapas, as a lateral narthex. The door of this narthex opens onto a stairway leading down to the plateau.

Thus the church, set against the hillside, colonnaded on one side and surrounded by chapels, makes up a picturesque group of buildings which owes its originality primarily to the contours of the ground. Its architecture could not follow the strictest forms, and its juxtaposition with the rock deprives it of the surrounding space which its proportions demand. Furthermore, the two eastern chapels hide the foundations of the church proper, making it seem to be suspended in the air.

44. The Peribleptos; south side.

SCULPTURED DECORATION

The sculptured decoration of the interior of the building, like most of the churches in Mystras, displays little homogeneity of style or execution. The upper moulding of the original iconostasis is still in place over the diaconicon; it is of the same workmanship and date as the moulding of the western chapel. Both seem to be re-used. The crowning mouldings on the north and south walls are decorated with a row of circular medallions containing a cross or a rosette; on the north there are also fleur-de-lys. Some details show that we are dealing with fragments taken from elsewhere and adapted to the new church.

45. *The Peribleptos; birth of the Virgin, north-west aisle.*

WALL PAINTINGS

The iconographic arrangement of scenes on the broad surfaces offered by the walls and vaults of the church does not present the clarity and simplicity which we find in the older churches such as the Metropolis, SS. Theodore and the Aphendiko.

Here, the three iconographic cycles, the Eucharistic, the Feasts, and the Passion scenes and the Life of the Virgin are interwoven. The Life of the Virgin, for example, begins in the western-northern vaults, continues and is developed in the double zone in the same vaults, proceeds further in the middle zone of the prothesis on the south wall of the low southern vault and ends in the diaconicon. The Gospel cycle begins with the Annunciation on the piers of the sanctuary, continues in the vaults of the three arms of the cross, is taken up in the lower zone of the vault of the diaconicon, with the Repentance of Peter and the Road to Calvary, and ends on the low southern vault with the Ascent to the Cross, the Crucifixion, the Descent of Christ from the Cross, the Holy Women at the Sepulchre and the Entombment. The Feasts occupy the chief place in the three high vaults, while the Passion cycle occupies a secondary position in the second zone of the west arm (the high vault) and the low southern vault. But the arrangement is conceived so that the large gables of the arms of the cross are occupied by the great and most important scenes in accordance with tradition: the Crucifixion (south), the Descent into Hell (west), and the Dormition of the Virgin above the entrance. It should be noted that the Life of the Virgin has here received exaggerated emphasis so that it has completely supplanted the Miracles.

The three apses are decorated with symbolic scenes. These include the Lamb of God (Amnos), the Communion of the Apostles, the Man of Sorrows and the Divine Liturgy and the Sleeping Emmanuel (Anapeson). There are also episodes from the Old Testament, including Abraham entertaining the Three Angels, the Sacrifice of Isaac and the Three Hebrews in the Fiery Furnace, three scenes relating to the mystery of the Eucharist, and there are many figures of prelates and saints, portrayed both full-length and as busts. In the conch of the apse the Virgin sits enthroned between two angels.

46. The Peribleptos; birth of Christ, south aisle. ▶

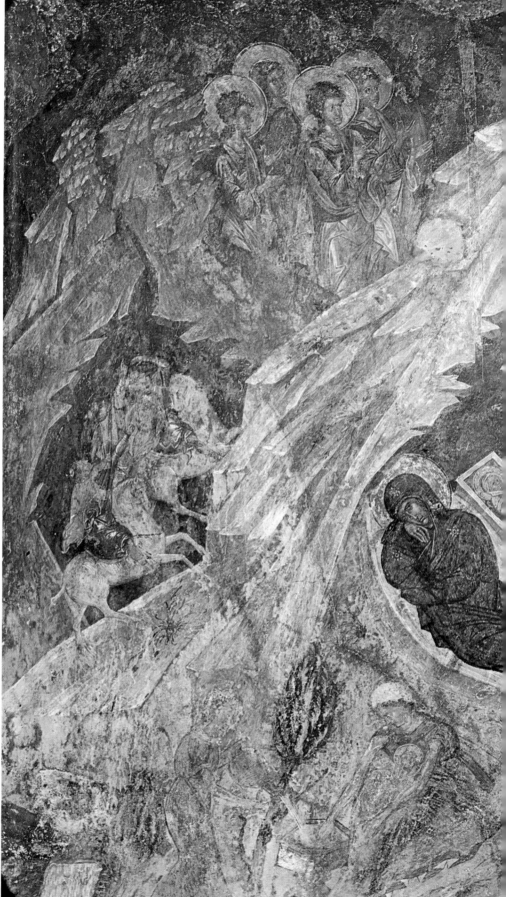

47. *The Peribleptos; the Pantocrator, Prophets, Virgin and the preparation of the Throne.*

The dome retains its decoration. The Pantacrator is in the centre; the remaining space is occupied by six pairs of Prophets, the Preparation of the Throne, *(Hetoimasia)* and the Virgin between two angels. The significance of these figures again relates to the Virgin; the Prophets are those who foretold her coming as the scrolls they hold makes clear.

On the side walls the lower zone has a row of youthful warrior saints standing life-size. On the pseudo-pilasters St. George and St. Demetrios are represented standing, more than life-size. On the west wall, in the niche, the two founders offer the church to the Virgin who is represented in the medallion above. Peter and Paul are on the pilasters of the same wall; below them, a narrow zone of imitation marble revetment runs around the whole church.

The paintings in the Peribleptos show greater unity of style than those of the other churches, so that they may be said to belong to one School and one period. If, however, the frescoes are examined very carefully, four different artists, or perhaps four different manners of painting, may be distinguished.

To one (A) we may attribute the Ascension (in the vault of the sanctuary), the

48. *The Peribleptos; prothesis, the angels from the Divine Liturgy.*

Dormition of the Virgin, the Transfiguration, the Resurrection of Lazarus, the Last Supper and the Entry into Jerusalem (in the vault of the west arm of the cross) and some figures of angels in the dome. The unique characteristic of this important painter is a fine feeling for pose, grace and quietness of action; even the excited Apostles in the Ascension, compared with the same scene in the Aphendiko, are peaceful and dignified. The artist is also characterized by another trait, a desire for symmetry; the Apostles form a group round the central figures of the Virgin and Angels. Finally, he is set apart by a conception of rhythm in motion, and in the disposition of space among the four superb angels who hover lightly around the central Glory in the Ascension. But he is also moved by picturesque detail. In the Entry into Jerusalem a crowd of children plays on the lower plane in the bottom part of the picture, and never did a crowd of Jews have such multi-coloured clothing. He can successfully relate large groups of figures. For the Dormition of the Virgin he chose a new type which was created in this period; from the left come angels, gentle idealized figures with richly dressed hair; the Apostles arrive on clouds, prelates stand by and a crowd of other persons follows the cen-

49. The Peribleptos; the Baptism, south aisle.

tral scene from the windows and balconies of innumerable symmetrical houses.

However, it is not colour that interests him most. The general tone is rather dark, and the background still darker. Side by side he uses light green, yellow and many shades of blue and red. The shadows in the drapery are formed by deeper tones of the same colour, varied by the occasional use of combinations such as wine-red with blue highlights. The faces are wheat-coloured with soft greenish shadows and delicate white highlights. The modelling thus becomes soft and round. The bodies seem to have no weight; they widen out at the waist, and stand rather insecurely on small delicate feet.

50. The Peribleptos; the Transfiguration, western aisle.

The same general characteristics were shared by another artist (B). To him we may attribute the Divine Liturgy in the prothesis, the Lamb of God in the sanctuary and the scenes from the Life of the Virgin in the north-west vault. Because of the rhythmical character of his compositions, there is greater emphasis on mysticism, which is especially apparent in the Divine Liturgy. The modelling attains great plasticity of form by the use of various shades of brown together with delicate white highlights. In the Descent from the Cross the heads of Christ and the women are of great beauty. The model for this scene, common also to Duccio, has been shown by Millet to be derived from an earlier Byzantine

51. The Peribleptos; The Entry to Jerusalem, west aisle.

prototype. The tone of the colours is the same as those used by painter A, but B makes greater use of blue and yellow. Both painters use red for mountains along with the complementary green.

To the third painter (C) we may attribute the Nativity, the Baptism on the south transverse vault, the Lament over the dead Christ, the Entombment, the Descent into Hell, the standing warrior saints in the lower zone, and the busts of saints in the double arched opening in the tympanum of the north transverse vault which looks into the cave-like women's gallery. The kinship of this painter with B is close; they are differentiated, however, by C's method of composition in which the landscape acquires greater significance than the individuals. This is especially clear in the Nativity and the Baptism. His tall slim figures are more delicate, and in general his tones are brighter. He differs also in the subdued melancholy given to his figures. As with B the modelling is tight, but it is distinguished from his by the fact that the delicate highlights radiate from the eyes instead of being parallel.

The fourth painter, (D), painted the Life of the Virgin in the lower northern

52. The Peribleptos; the Procession to Golgotha, diaconicon.
53. The Peribleptos; the Doubting of Thomas, north aisle.

84

vault. There is a different atmosphere here, more intimate, with more movement, and showing a certain hastiness of plan and execution. There are many buildings in his pictures, and small graceful figures move quickly among them in bold ex-

54. The Peribleptos; the Dormition of the Virgin, north side.

aggerated poses. A frequent motif is the stairway leading up to a building, or similar subjects which show that, although the rendering may not be entirely succesful, there was an underlying conception of depth and space.

55. The Peribleptos; St. John the Baptist, south wall.

A completely different tendency, though possibly related to this painter, can be distinguished in at least five scenes in the diaconicon; the Repentance of Peter, the Road to Calvary, the Ascent to the Cross, the *Anapeson* and some of the figures of bishops. These scenes, which are not separated from each other as the others are, are characterized by the obvious lack of grace in the stance of the figures and lack of nobility in their gestures. This emphatic brutality of action is also expressed by an exaggeration of pose and the ugliness of their faces. These realistic

56. The Peribleptos; warrior saints on the north wall.

trends sharply distinguish this small group of paintings from the rest of the work of the Peribleptos.

The wall paintings of this church, rich in iconography, varied in artistic manner and marked by the high standard of painting, are to be counted equal to the most representative works of the best traditions of the capital in the third quarter of the 14th century Its conservatism is expressed by the return to the high standard of the models of the first period of the 14th century such as the Kariye Djami.

THE EVANGELISTRIA

In the Middle Town, on the road between the Metropolis and the Brontochion, stands the little church of the Evangelistria. Its churchyard is still used as a cemetery. The Evangelistria is the only church in Mystras without any recorded history: there are no documents, no inscriptions and no portrait either of its founder or of its re-builder. It is a most melancholy monument, surrounded by the tombs and bone-pits of the men who lived in the now dead city. A few dated graffiti on the walls show only that the church was not desecrated by the Turks; one in the prothesis reads "Nikephoros priest-monk of Athens, 1633", and another of 1711 "Gregorios priest-monk, took the Ach....". Carved on the north wall of the sanctuary in fine letters of the 15th century we read "Phrantzis". Can this be the historian?

ARCHITECTURE

The Evangelistria, like the Peribleptos and St. Sophia, belongs to the two-column cross-in-square type church. Its dimensions are smaller than those of the other two churches, but the proportions inside are graceful and spacious. Outside, there is little decoration; the high apses lack even a row of brick saw-tooth, though both the five-sided central apse and the three-sided lateral apses are pierced by a two-lobed window. The *cloisonné* masonry, confined to the east end, the arms of the cross and the drum of the dome, is not faultlessly executed, and it succeeds only in emphasizing the significance of each architectural member. The eight-sided drum of the dome has four windows alternating with four niches. The windows are crowned by double arches supported by short columns, most of which are now missing. The single remaining gable, in the north arm of the cross, contrasts strongly with the plastic quality of the drum of the dome. It has a two-lobed window surrounded by rich ornamental brickwork, resembling that in St. Sophia. A further resemblance to St. Sophia is the height of the apses which is equal to the height of the eastern end of the cross, as it is also in the Aphendiko, from which church the Evangelistria also copied a feature which we find in no other church of the two-column type: a narthex with a women's gallery. Its roof

57. The Evangelistria; south-east view.

has not survived, but it is clear that it was covered by a vault. The stairway which led to the women's gallery was supported by a small room added onto the south side of the church, and used as an ossuary. This was continued by a small colonnade, with two arches and one column. The tympanum of a large arch with rich ornamental brickwork crowning a double arch is preserved on the west wall of the churchyard. It is at a much lower level than the church, and is probably the remains of a second colonnade which ran the length of the west wall of the churchyard. West of the narthex, at a lower level, is a spacious vaulted chamber like an exo-narthex, almost certainly a later ossuary since it was found full of bones. The north side of the church which is built in the usual masonry is of no special interest. There were originally two doors; the older of these is now blocked up, the other, arched and with carved decoration, is open.

SCULPTURED DECORATION

The carvings display a uniformity of style which proves that they are the original decoration and integral with the church. They are therefore an interesting example of decorative sculpture, rare in Mystras. The almost square capitals are unique. The ornate leaf design is carved in low relief. Above this, smooth bosses in the shape of pine cones project at the corners. The loose composition resembles an imitation of textile design, such as folk embroidery. Between the branches, geometric patterns are combined with crosses. On the impost blocks of the capitals and pseudo-pilasters there are motifs which we have met in the other churches: palmettes had rinceaux. The iconostasis, now blocked up, must originally have had three doors decorated with carved frames. Today, only the central door preserves its frame, which shows strong western influence in its shape, its rhomboidal ornament and in the carving of the last saw-tooth towards the middle. This feature is often found in Cretan churches built in the Venetian style. The lintel of the iconostasis has an interlace decoration. Three bosses project above this, set close together, and the lintel terminates in pine cones at each end. The exterior lintel of the north door of the church, which is too narrow for the door, is decorated in the same style, having been taken either from the diaconicon or the prothesis. Earlier carving is found only on the mullions of the two-lobed windows and the column of the south colonnade.

WALL PAINTINGS

The scanty remains of wall paintings on the Evangelistria frustrate attempts to restore the iconographic arrangement in detail. However, from what is preserved, it seems that this differs little from the schemes of St. Sophia and the Peribleptos. Traces of angels under an arcade of trefoil pointed arches of the later Gothic type have been preserved in the dome. Low down in the sanctuary is the Lamb of God, and above it was the Communion of the Apostles. The Ascension was probably in the vault. Fragments from the life of the Virgin can be seen in the diaconicon, while the prothesis was decorated with angels holding fans.

The paintings are in the Palaiologue tradition as developed at Mystras to emphasize the qualities of elegance and graceful motion. The drawing, however, is very weak and rather provincial, leaving the impression that it is the mechanical repetition of good prototypes. The well preserved figure of the prelate, St. Polykarpos, found on the inner surface of the arch which leads from the

58. Partial view of the ruined city of Mystras.

sanctuary to the prothesis, was executed in almost monochrome shading from brown to ochre against a green background. The Evangelist in the north-west pendentive, whose green garment has shadows of light brown with light green high-lights, is more interesting from the point of view of colour.

The Evangelistria should probably be dated to the beginning of the 15th century rather than to the end of the 14th because its construction, sculpture and painting point to a period which imitates the finer earlier examples without achieving their beauty.

THE PANTANASSA

The Monastery of the Pantanassa was built in a commanding position on a steep slope on the east side of the mountain. It is clearly visible from all directions, an unmistakeably medieval building with its six-domed church, lofty bell-tower and elegant colonnade. It is the best preserved of all the monuments in Mystras, and the nuns who inhabit it still keep alive the medieval tradition of hospitality.

It was founded by John Phrangopoulos, the chief minister of the Despotat, whose name and titles are to be found painted on the arches of the west facade and in relief on the capital of the south-west column of the church: "The founder John Phrangopoulos, protostrator and katholikos mesazon". The foundation of the church by this important personage was also recorded in a metrical inscription around the base of the dome of the narthex.

Another inscription now lost, but copied by the French traveller Fourmont from the altar slab, conveys the rather confusing information about the date of the foundation, that the dedication of "the imperial and patriarchal monastery of the all-holy Theotokos, called Pantanassa" took place in September 1428.

On the base of the bell-tower in the court monograms inscribed in a circle read "Constantine Kavratzakes November 17 of the year 7080 (=1571). It would seem that the grammarian Kavratzakes was buried here and a tomb erected to his memory. Another tomb was found along the south wall of the narthex, where the nobleman Manuel Lascaris Chatzikes was buried, according to the monogram on the *arcosolium* and traces of an inscription beside his portrait gives the date of his death (6953=1445).

59. The Pantanassa; view from the south-west.

There seems to be no reason to accept the identification of the Pantanassa with the "Zoodotes Monastery" which we know from texts and seals to have been founded by the Despot Manuel Katakouzenos. Supposing that he was indeed the founder, the work of Phrangopoulos would have been merely repair or renovation, carried out barely 50-60 years after the erection of the building. Of such a re-building there is no trace. Moreover, the monograms of Phrangopoulos are found in the places usually reserved for those of the founder of the church or monastery (such as the impost blocks) so that the inference is not unreasonable. There are, however, other difficulties in the way of ascribing the foundation to Katakouzenos. The chronicle assumed to have been written by one Phrantzis says that the bones of Theodora Tokkou, wife of Constantine Palaiologos, who died in St. Omer in 1429 were brought to this monastery, and that the wife of Theodore Palaiologos, Kleopa Malatesta, who died in 1433, was also buried here. We have seen, however, that by 1428 the monastery had been dedicated in the name of the Pantanassa.

ARCHITECTURE

The western entrance of the monastery, once monumental, but no longer standing complete, leads into a long narrow court. From there, two steps ascend to a small artificial platform on which the church is built. The contours of the ground compelled the architect to orient the building on an axis approximately north-south. The plan of the church is faithful to the model of the Aphendiko, a three aisled basilica below, a five-domed cross-in-square church above. The only real difference is in the proportions, for by this time the feeling for rhythmic proportion had been lost and the arrangement of the interior space lacks the harmony of the prototype.

The apses, as in the Aphendiko, are very high, but their exterior decoration is richer and more sophisticated. Two cornices divide the surface into three zones, of which the lower and narrower is innocent of decoration as in the Metropolis and elsewhere. The other two zones have a continuous row of windows, one open window alternating with one blind window. In the upper zone the large arched windows are divided by little columns which support semi-circular arches. The middle, wider zone repeats the same theme in a different style. The windows are narrower and more numerous; the arches which surround them are Gothic and have rinceaux above them. Up to the upper cornice the surface is filled with a garland in relief like an inverted arcade, corresponding exactly to the Gothic arches. The juxtaposition of these two zones, which have no relation to each other stylistically, show how little interest there was by this time in unity, and that the preference was for decorative eclecticism. Porches with symmetrical arches dominate the other sides. The only decoration on the exposed surfaces was the *cloisonné masonry* emphasizing the chief members; the piers, arches and drums of the domes. Saw-tooth courses adorn the apses here and continue onto the long sides.

The Frankish influence is even more apparent in the sturdy bell-tower which rises four storeys above the court. This tower is built entirely in *cloisonné masonry,* but its three-lobed window openings are bordered by a large "Gothic" arch. On two sides it has small trefoil openings in a circular frame like those in the tower of the Peribleptos. Small four towers flank the small melon dome on top. Here we encounter more Frankish influence than in any of the other buildings in Mystras, yet the proportions of the bell-tower are carefully worked out so that it

60. *The Pantanassa; the monastery from the west; the castle above.*

is a harmonious complement to the main building. The bell-tower is an integral part of the church connecting the two open porches around the church. That in front of the narthex has not survived; the northern porch, however, is preserved intact. It is the only example in Mystras to have remained undamaged. It preserves its colonnades roofed with low vaults, with a rather higher dome in the middle. From the colonnade there is a superb view over the valley of the Eurotas.

The entire building is in a good state of preservation. The dome of the church itself is more recent; of the original dome only a part towards the north remains together with the beginning of the fluting on the interior.

The Pantanassa is a brilliant example of the architecture of Mystras at the beginning of the 15th century. Local design is still apparent in the plan and older elements in the decoration: along with other, newer decorative elements derived from the Franks, three traditions have been assimilated into a united whole. The weakness and the eclecticism which, as we noted before, characterized the architecture of this period, do not diminish the historical and artistic value of this monument in either its architectural or its decorative aspects. Here, good taste, powerful composition and spiritual expression place it in the best Byzantine tradition.

SCULPTURED DECORATION

The sculpture decoration exhibits the same variety which we have met in other buildings. This does not mean, however, that the different fragments necessarily come from different periods of this building, since much has been re-used from elsewhere.

The column capitals in the interior are of three kinds, and are to be dated to different periods: one has spear-shaped leaves similar to the style found in the Metropolis; two capitals, more conical in outline, resemble a developed form of Corinthian style with acanthus at the base and small unaccentuated spirals; three others, more cubical, have a more marked plasticity with acanthus at the base and strong spirals with a large rosette in the centre. They are all smaller than the impost blocks. Of these, three a rinceau in relief with a cross in the middle, while the fourth, in place of the cross, has the circular monogram of the Phrangopouloi. The other two impost blocks appear to be unworked. The carved impost blocks are contemporary with the construction of the church, as are also the three capitals of the exterior colonnade which are carved in low relief and are inspired by the capitals of the interior. On the string course at the spring of the vaults is an elaborate rinceau, and another, at the base of the main dome, is carved in higher relief, more coarsely executed.

The doorway leading from the narthex to the church proper is interesting in that it shows motifs of an Islamic character; pseudo-cufic decoration and rinceaux with long half-leaves elegantly executed in low relief. There are other sculptures from the Pantanassa. They include a fine eagle with outspread wings (from the iconostasis of the monastery) which is now in the Museum; an arch with two eagles built into the church of St. George in New Mystras and other fragments in different styles. The realistic rendering of the eagles, in sharp contrast to the usual sculptural style at Mystras, should probably be attributed to the work of foreign craftsmen.

Near the church, a sculptural plaque with the monogram of the Katakouzenoi was found. It is now in the Museum, but it cannot be connected with the history of the monastery.

61. *The Pantanassa; the exterior decoration on the sanctuary apses and the stoa.*

WALL PAINTINGS

The original wall decoration has survived in fairly good condition in the arms of the cross and in the upper storey. Poorly preserved paintings of the 17th and early 18th centuries are to be found on the lower floor. On the north-west and south walls are representations of the twenty-four strophes (*oikoi*) of the Akathistos Hymn and various saints while in the narthex are martyrdoms. From the original decoration here only the figure of St. Mary of Egypt survives.

The iconographic arrangement corresponds to that of the Aphendiko. On the vaults of the arms of the cross is the cycle of Feasts: the Annunciation and the Nativity on the south arm, the Presentation and the Baptism on the west, the Transfiguration and the Raising of Lazarus on the north, the Entry into Jerusalem and the Descent into Hell on the east. The Ascension occupies the entire vault of the sanctuary. In the tympana of the arches of the cross are Gospel scenes of secondary importance: on the south the Flight into Egypt, on the west Christ teaching in the Temple and on the north Christ surrounded by the Apostles. The Evangelists are painted in the pendentives, but around the drum of the

62. The Pantanassa; the Flight into Egypt, south tympanum.

101

dome decoration has been lost. The Seventy Apostles were painted on the flat surfaces of the gallery and the Prophets and Patriarchs with Cherubim in the saucer domes. In the drums of the smaller domes are figures of standing Prophets while in the sanctuary, the figure of the Virgin, enthroned between two archangels, has been preserved. Joachim and Anna stand below her. The remaining scenes in the sanctuary are contemporary with those on the ground floor. The Passion cycle and the Miracles of Jesus are both missing. These too must originally have been on the lower floor, and perhaps also in the narthex.

In iconographic details the scenes painted often follow faithfully the depiction to be found in the Peribleptos, for example in the Raising of Lazarus and the Entry into Jerusalem, although they reflect the contemporary traditions. In its style, however, the school of artists which painted the Pantanassa was eclectic. It was much influenced by the Aphendiko, mainly in its endeavour to give volume to the cylindrical bodies, in the detail it gave to the imposing faces of the aged and in the rocky landscapes. Inspired by the Peribleptos, it imitated a love of picturesque detail, and presented intimate scenes with a scene of movement in the crowds.

This eclecticism necessarily makes a difference in the scenes, but one hesitates to attribute pictures to individual painters. The Ascension and the Virgin (Platytera) both have a monumental quality, especially perhaps the Ascension, where the composition has the symmetry we find in the Peribleptos. Here, the plastic figures move with restraint, standing firmly on uneven ground. The colours are brilliant, and the shadows are shown in deeper tones of the same colours. The modelling of the body is soft, with many shadows and delicate white highlights. In the scene of the Annunciation, the colouring is extremely delicate; the angel finds the Virgin in a garden with a red fence beside a fountain where partridges are drinking. The background is filled with complex buildings with porphyry columns. In the Nativity, the green ground with red-brown shadows and fissures is the most striking feature. The alternation of concave and convex surfaces, the many curves and corners, provide an uneasy and somewhat discordant appearance. In the Presentation the human figures are smaller than in the other drawings. They stand in front of a red-walled three storeyed building which unfolds in depth and height with canopies and balconies in yellow-green and with some red walls.

A completely different spirit governs the scene of the Raising of Lazarus where groups of figures move slowly in a quiet place. On the right hand side the ground is shown as a broad yellow surface on which a green-clothed Jew stands, holding his nose ("by now he stinks" John 11.39). At the head of a compact group is a blue-clothed Christ and to the left, scarcely discernible, are greenish mountains, and the buildings seen through the rocks, are aubergine coloured. The crowds lend a slow rhythmic movement to the impressive setting of the scene. The space by the intersecting rocks is emphasized by the figures and by the perspective of the buildings. The Lazarus scene is related to the preceding episodes by similarities in style, for example the impressionistic modelling of the faces with very delicately drawn white highlights and particular colour combinations, such as a grey-blue garment with chocolate brown folds and outlines. These renderings could lead us to attribute the Annunciation, the Nativity, the Presentation, the Baptism, the Transfiguration, the Raising of Lazarus and the Evangelists painted on the pendentives to a single painter. The Entry to Jerusalem is related in spirit to the Raising of Lazarus; it has, however, more polychromy and a great variety

63. The Pantanassa; detail from the Ascension in the vault of the sanctuary.

of scenes treated in detail in composition of the buildings and generally in the treatment of space. The children scattered about below connect the lower with the main level where a hurrying group of Jews clothed in multi-coloured garments moves in counter-balance to the small peaceful group of Christ and his disciples. Of the Descent into Hell only the lower right-hand section is well-preserved, with its sarcophagi shown in perspective and painted in bright colours; wine-red, almost green, violet and grey-green, all clear and blending tones. The rocks have been very carefully worked in broad bright planes above the olive green ground. In the Journey to Bethlehem Joseph's extremely tall silhouette is combined with the life-like rendering of the donkey, while the features of the faces indicate a lively discussion in progress.

The Seventy Apostles round the walls of the gallery are close to the corresponding figures in the Aphendiko : they differ, however, both in the use of colour (the complementary tones are lacking here) and in the simplicity and relax-ation of the earlier figures. Here, the sophisticated drapery is very carefully thought out and the broad highlights move in a continuous pattern, so that the folds acquire a quasi-rigidity. This diminishes the rhythmic effect of the drapery

64. The Pantanassa; the Birth of Christ, south aisle.

65. *The Pantanassa; the Virgin and the manger, detail from the Birth of Christ.*

66. The Pantanassa; the Entry to Jerusalem, east aisle.

which was so well exploited by the painter of the Aphendiko. But in spite of this, the plasticity and weight of the bodies is emphatically expressed so that these figures recall ancient sculpture. The Apostles in the Ascension are very closely related to the Seventy, both in the general conception of the figures and in the technical details. The artists who drew the somewhat flabby Prophets on the ceiling were less skilful.

Although the scenes and groups of scenes differ from each other, they have one general characteristic which gives homogeneity to the paintings of the Pantanassa. This is a strongly emphasized mannerism revealed both in the entire

67. The Pantanassa; the Entry to Jeusalem, detail.

composition and in the details of scenes. It is a mannerism which produces nothing of its own, but re-works known methods and often accentuates secondary elements, so breaking the unity of composition and of space and still more, the narrative interest of the main scene. This finnicky breaking-up, technically fault-less, characterizes the last tired period of Palaiologue painting.

The paintings in the Pantanassa are of high quality. They can be dated with reasonable certainty to about 1430. We can well understand from them why the art of this period, and particularly the tendency which they represent, survived into the 16th and 17th centuries along with the work of the Cretan School.

68. St. George; view from the south.

THE CHAPELS

In addition to its large churches Mystras has at least twenty small private chapels, primarily funerary in character. With the exception of St. Paraskeve, which is a cross-in-square church, these are small barrel-vaulted structures with cisterns or other structures attached. All have many tombs, both inside and out-side, which have been used and re-used many times. These out of the way buildings have gradually crumbled and some have been covered with earth. In the years after the Second World War they have been carefully cleared of the ac-cumulation of earth and debris, and the two most characteristic, St. George and St. Christopher, have been re-built and their frescoes restored. Minor reconstruc-tion work in the others has made the general lines clear, and has uncovered some sections of the frescoed decoration and a few dated inscriptions.

The identification of the chapels is somewhat arbitrary. To those which still retain the form of a church, local tradition has assigned names which are still in use today.

AI YANNAKIS (ST. JOHN)

Outside the wall, near Marmara, is a small barrel-vaulted church which suffered in earlier restorations. Some frescoes of the 15th century, interesting for their iconographic originality, may still be distinguished. The best, which are on the east wall above the iconostasis, show traces of the Annunciation which is presented in conjunction with the Virgin as the Life-Giving Source (Zoodochos Pigi), executed in a free style with picturesque details. Some parts of a many-figured Crucifixion scene may also be made out, noteworthy for the pronounced curve in the body of the dead Christ; there is also the Last Supper, with the new semi-circular arrangement of the figures; the Doubting of Thomas and the Ascension.

A Prophet in the arch of the sanctuary, painted with a certain amount of freedom, has green shadows on a yellow-brown face, and blue highlights on the hair and beard.

In the west apse of the south wall the founder is portrayed, "the Lady Kali Kavalasea who, by divine intention became a nun and was re-named Kalliniki, with her children". As Kali, she is represented wearing a white kerchief and a blue dress, while as Kalliniki she wears the monastic black. Her daughter, Lascarina, and her son, Hodegetrianos, both wear red.

ST. GEORGE

St. George, near the Peribleptos, is a gracefully proportioned little building with a lateral adjoining narthex which has been restored.

Of the other chapels, we should note St Anna and St Kyriake, the latter still preserving part of its frescoed Baptism.

ST. CHRISTOPHER

Not far away, on the road leading from the Peribleptos to the Metropolis, is the chapel of St. Christopher which has been restored. It preserves a few fine frescoes, including St. Chrysostom enthroned; in the arch are Apostles surrounding the youthful figure of a saint with unruly hair, possibly St. Christopher. The style is related to that of the Peribleptos, although some of the figures are rather more mannered or schematic. For this reason they may be dated around the end of the 14th century.

THE PALACE CHAPEL

Near the open square of the palace a hitherto unknown chapel was recently uncovered containing the remains of fine wall paintings. On the north wall is a series of warrior saints graceful, slender figures which are not far removed either chronologically or stylistically from those of the Peribleptos.

THE CASTLE CHAPEL

Finally, in a double chapel in the inner keep of the castle, there are a few wall paintings which appear to be among the oldest in Mystras. The figure of a hierarch may be made out.

69. The Palaces and the central square.

THE PALACE

In the *plateia* of the Upper City a large complex of buildings is preserved. Tourists during the Turkish Occupation naively identified these with the "Palace of Menelaos", and popular tradition calls them "the Palace of the Princess". These massive buildings form two wings joined nearly at a right-angle at the northern point of the square thus closing the west and east side of the rectangular *plateia*. The open space faced towards the sun and away from the wind, and it was sufficiently large for all public gatherings which might take place under the protection of the authorities.

The buildings were not all constructed at the same time. The first to be erected was the end of the east wing which has a few windows, of which those in the upper row have pointed Gothic arches. This section may have been built by the Franks (1249-1261), or by the first Greek governors, because it resembles other Frankish buildings of the Morea such as Chlemoutsi. The kitchen was built at the same time, with its fireplace and cisterns. Another building was erected to connect the other two. This is contemporary with a two storey building on the other side of the kitchen with six spacious rooms on each floor — the residence of the Despot and his family. Its north side (now restored) is interesting, with a open porch supported by five piers and decorated above the piers with a series of the small arches characteristic of the civil buildings of Byzantine Mystras. The roof of this porch forms a balcony from which the nobles could enjoy the view of the valley. The door leading to the balcony has stone jambs and, to judge from the existing fragments, they were of late Gothic Venetian type.

The middle room of the upper storey was transformed into a chapel with an apse and wall paintings, of which only traces survive. The residential building which for architectural reasons is dated to the years 1350-1400, completes the north-east wing. The north-west wing is adjacent, and consists of a single large building. This building has a half-cellar with a vaulted ceiling and a low first floor with eight apartments unconnected with each other, each covered with a semi-cylindrical vault. Above this was the second storey, consisting of a single lofty hall, the "chysotriklinon" (the Golden Throne Room) of the Byzantines, measuring 36.30m in length and 10.50m. in width. On its east side is a row of windows with late Gothic frames, and a second row of six round windows; a projecting niche in the middle of the wall accommodated the throne. Round the room on the inside ran a low bench where visitors could sit. This spacious room was heated by

70. *The throne room in the palace of the Palaiologoi.*

eight fireplaces, the flues of which pass through the west wall and jut out from the exterior face like buttresses. Seen from the *plateia,* the chief characteristic of this wing is its large two-storeyed porch, corresponding with the two storeys of the building. Its roof forms a sort of balcony. The porch lightens the building, and at the same time adds a picturesque touch to the great unbroken surface of the facade. Only the bases of several of the exterior piers which supported this porch have been preserved, found during excavation. In the 17th century it was already in a ruinous condition, and learned travellers identified it with the "Persian Stoa" of Ancient Sparta.

The walls of both wings are built of rubble masonry. The wall of the older wing contains more carefully dressed stone, so that it is probable that it was not plastered. The exterior wall of the north-west wing, however, still retains traces of plaster which must have concealed its cheap construction. Over the light-coloured plaster narrow horizontal red bands imitate brick. The interior wall was also plastered, and in the throne room at least there must have been wall paintings.

The older, north-east wing, gives an agreeable impression of plasticity with the stepped articulation of its buildings. It has at the same time a decidedly fortress-

71. Detail of a window in the palace with a pointed arch.

72. *View of the palace complex from above; right, the wing of the Katakouzenoi*

73. *Partial view of the Palaiologue palace.*

like character with its small widely spaced windows and its tower-like sections. The north-west wing of the Palaiologue period with its simple mass, its impressive porch and the austere arrangement of the many large windows, has, on the other hand a monumental quality which shows evidence of wealth and power. In plan and construction it has many analogies with Byzantine buildings, such as the so-called Palace of the Porphyrogenitos (Tekfour Serai) of the 13th-14th centuries in Constantinople. In the decoration of the large windows, however, as well as in the circular form of the upper row, it recalls early Renaissance palaces of Italy. This wing must have been built after 1400 by the Palaiologoi, and it seems that it was burnt down in the attack of Sigismund Malatesta in 1464, a short time after the fall of the Despotat (1460). A small higher building contiguous to the palace is older.

The north-east wing was built near the wall which surrounds the terrace, leaving only a narrow road between. To the west of the other wing, however, was a fairly large space where other buildings were erected, probably for the use of court officials or other nobles.

74. *Another view of the palace.*

75. *Partial view of the palace, with one wing built by Katakouzenoi (right) and the other by the Palaiologoi (left).*

THE HOUSES

The general form of the houses was determined by the steep and uneven contours of the hill, and by the urban character which Mystras acquired. On the fortified side of the hill, the space was small for the flourishing capital of the Despotat, and it did not afford room for spacious courts and gardens. The narrow streets led diagonally towards the declivity, and for that reason the houses were oriented more or less on a lateral axis. Moreover, a house had to have more than one storey, because the ground floor was underground at the back. Thus the houses developed a long rectangular shape and stood contiguous to each other. In only a few cases was there a small court. Chateaubriand, at the beginning of the 19th century, saw many gardens in Mystras, but it must not be forgotten that by that time the population had greatly decreased, and thus space had been acquired for gardens. Usually, the long side of the house ran parallel to the hillside. The large houses fall into three types: a) the simplest and most common, two storeys without a tower; b) a veranda on the facade looking towards the valley; c) and d) the real mansions with a strong tower built to protect the house.

The family led its life on the first, or upper, floor, while the lower, or ground floor was used as a store-room or stable, with narrow openings instead of windows for reasons of security. Often, part of the vaulted ground floor, the "diavaticon", was used for transients. The upper floor consisted of one spacious room, the "triklinon", with large windows all round and many niches which served as cupboards.

The houses often had balconies which projected or were formed by part of the roof of the lower storey. In either case, the front of the balcony was supported by a row of decorative small arches. These have been considered to be of Genoese origin, but they are actually found in buildings of Constantinople earlier than in those of Mystras. Furthermore, they have survived in later popular architecture in the Morea.

The buildings were supported by a system of large arches on both storeys. With this system, the walls which fill the arches can be made lighter, (an economic factor), the building can stand more firmly on the uneven ground, (a structural factor) and there are thus created plastic values which give character to the buildings (an aesthetic factor). All the openings are arched, or are surrounded by an arched lintel. Thus the arch constitutes the principle element in the houses of Mystras.

76. One of the houses of Mystras.

77. *The ruins of the House of Lascaris.*

78. *Reconstruction drawing of the House of Lascaris.*

The roof was always gabled; a vaulted roof would have been very heavy, while the severe winter conditions made a flat roof impracticable.

A few houses have been preserved in relatively good condition. The oldest and largest is in the City of Mystras, a little above St. Nicholas. It has been called the "little palace" or the "mansion". As it stands today, it is the most composite house in Mystras, because, as Professor Orlandos has shown, it consists of two buildings of different periods; the northern with the tower is older, the southern later. It has three storeys, but the older part has large windows only on the second floor, and on the ground floor and middle storey, which is very low, it has narrow openings.

Also of importance is the so-called "House of Phrangopoulos", which lies below the Pantanassa and towards the Peribleptos. On its northern facade, above the balcony, were two large arched openings; the present rectangular windows are unskilful earlier restoration. It had underground cisterns, and its roof was gabled. It must have been built about the beginning of the 15th century.

A similar house is the "House of Lascaris" near the Metropolis. The small ground floor with its vaulted ceiling was perhaps a stable. The first floor was low, and had a large semi-circular opening in front, above which was a balcony.

Mystras preserves the best examples of Byzantine city houses known to us, and it is here that we may look for many elements which have survived to characterize modern Greek popular domestic architecture.

THE CITADEL AND THE WALLS

From the gate to the south of the Nauplia Gate, a steep cobbled road leads to the citadel on the summit of the hill, the spot chosen by Villehardouin for his stronghold. In its present form it retains very little of the original construction, for the continuous work of preservation, first by the Byzantines and later by the Turks, has re-built it almost entirely.

The citadel encloses a flat space, and is defended by two circuits, an inner and an outer. The entrance to the outer enclosure is vaulted and a conspicuous square tower stands beside it. In this area, which is a little lower but larger than the inner enclosure, are ruins of houses of the Turkish period. At the south-east end, near a large cistern, is a round tower for the sentries. From there it was possible to overlook the entire plain and the slopes of Taygetos. On this side, as well on the side which looks towards Taygetos, the hillside rock of Mystras drops almost vertically, making the citadel inaccessible.

The north-west part of the plateau is higher, and is surrounded by a second stronger enclosure wall. This area constitutes the keep, and contains, to the left of the entrance, a large building which served as the residence of the successive governors of the citadel. Nearby are the ruins of a chapel. At the west end stands another sentry-post which overlooks the western slopes of Taygetos from which the savage Melingi might attack.

The citadel was the chief point in the defensive system, and the city walls

79. The castle on the top of the hill.

extended the area which it commanded. Here, too, are two circuits. The first and oldest started westwards from the citadel and continued downwards; it embraced the plateau where the palace lay and continued above the Pantanassa as far as the precipice. Its western side, which was the strongest, consisted of successive massive towers, both square and round. The two gates on this side were especially heavily fortified with flanking towers.

The second and later enclosure has as its north-west boundary the Aphendiko, its north-east the Metropolis and as its south-east the Peribleptos. It was indeed apparently created for the protection of these three monasteries.

The remains of the walls of both circuits are considerable and impressive.

THE MYTH OF MYSTRAS

When Cyriacus of Ancona, a restlessly adventurous antiquarian, came to Mystras about 1447, he reflected with melancholy that the glorious Sparta of Lykourgos, the Dioskouroi and Leonidas had ended up as the wretched Mystras of Constantine Palaiologos, and he wrote an epigram very unflattering to his protector, the Despot of Mystras.

This poetic linking of Mystras with Sparta affected western ideas about the capital of the Despotat to such an extent that Mystras was thought to have been built on the very site of Ancient Sparta, and certain of its buildings were thought to be those of antiquity.

This confusion had not yet arisen in the time of Cyriacus of Ancona who accurately described the ruins of Ancient Sparta. Nor was it felt by the condottieri Sigismund Malatesta when, in 1461, he took with him the remains of Gemistos, "the most wise philosopher whose fame is next to that of Aristotle" (as the chronographer of Rimini writes) in order to deposit them near the tombs of the other wise men of his court. Gemistos still shed his special lustre on Mystras.

By the 17th century, however, the identification of the two cities had become general. Among those responsible for this were travellers and antiquarians such as de la Guilletières (Guillet) who, without having set foot in the Morea, vividly described the place and the people. He recognised the Palace of Menelaos, as he also recognised the ancient Laconian character and customs in the life of the inhabitants of Lacedaemonia, not only of Greeks, but of Turks also. Nevertheless, Guillet was able to appreciate Byzantine monuments, and he notes that if there are ten fine churches in the world, the Peribleptos is one.

Again, these travellers, as well as the geographers who based their work on them, such as Coronelli and others, influenced the most cultured inhabitants of Mystras who were flattered by the identification. An Appendix to the Chronograph, a popular work attributed to Dorotheos of Monemvasia, gave widespread distribution to the same legend. Even in 1798 the citizen of Mystras who accompanied Pouqueville as a guide, fitted all the topography of Ancient Sparta to Mystras, and the Frenchman was inclined to believe him.

It took Chateaubriand, passing through this vicinity on a journey from Paris to Jerusalem in 1806 to realize that Sparta and Mystras were two different places.

80. Gate of the Citadel. 81. The Monemvasia Gate.

He asserted later (1827) that he had made no new discovery, since early travellers, such as Spon, Vernon, Leroi, Fourmont and others had never had any doubt of it. From that time Mystras regained its identity.

Mystras acquired a new significance in the cultural history of Europe with the Helen of Goethe's second Faust (1824). Guided by his sure instinct, the poet of Weimar endowed Mystras with symbolic significance as the spot where classical beauty, as exemplified by Helen, united with romantic chivalry, Faust, to give birth to Euphorion, who is heedless of whether he himself may not be sacrificed to the idea of liberty.

The accuracy of Goethe's description of the locality is impressive:

> *So many years deserted stood the valley hills*
> *That in the rear of Sparta northwards rise aloft*
> *Behind Taygetos: whence, as yet a nimble brook,*
> *Eurotas downward rolls, and then along our vale*
> *By reed beds broadly flowing, nourishes your swans.*
> *Behind there in the mountain dwells a daring breed*
> *Have settled, pressing forth from the Cimmerian Night,*
> *And there have built a fortress inaccessible,*
> *Whence land and people now they harry as they please.*

For these descriptions of the natural features of the place he must have been helped by recent travellers, such as the Englishmen Gell (1823) who gives a correct lithograph of Mystras, and others whom we know the poet consulted at that time. He was fully familiar with all details of the Frankish Occupation. It is believed (G. Moracik and N. Bees) that Goethe used the chronographer Pseudo — Dorotheos, because the Chronicle of the Morea was still unpublished in 1824. The chronographer's phrase about the Greek wife of William II Villehardouin "most beautiful and gracious from her head to her whole body, like a second Helen of Menelaos" must have seemed especially suggestive to the poet.

Goethe's conception has had a lamentable influence on more recent visitors to Mystras. Even Maurice Barrès in his "Journey to Sparta" sees in Mystras nothing but the scene of the second Faust. He is dominated by the prestige of Helen and Euphorion. He hardly recalls his ancestor, Villehardouin, and the Byzantines are a matter of complete indifference to him.

It was French scholarship which finally restored to the citadel, founded by medieval Frenchmen, its true significance which through the body of its Byzantine monuments brought both the artistic importance and the historical importance of the city into full view. For the student of Byzantine art and civilisation Mystras provides unique material, and for all travellers it provides the best single visual link between medieval and modern Greece.

BIBLIOGRAPHY

CHATZIDAKIS, M., *Μυστρᾶς*, Athens, 1956.
   —Ἡ ζωγραφική στό Μυστρᾶ, *Ἀγγλο-Ἑλληνική Ἐπιθεώρησις*, Athens, 1953.
   —Νεώτερα ἀπό τή Μητρόπολη τοῦ Μυστρᾶ (with a summary in french), *Δελτίον Χριστιανικῆς Ἀρχαιολογικῆς Ἑταιρείας*, 1977-79.
DELVOYE, CH., *Mistra, Corci di cultura sull'arte ravennate e bizantina*, Ravenna, 1964.
DRANDAKIS, M., Ἀνασκαφές στά παρεκκλήσια τοῦ Μυστρᾶ, *Πρακτικά τῆς Ἀρχαιολογικῆς Ἑταιρείας*, Athens, 1952.
   —Τοιχογραφίες στά παρεκκλήσια τοῦ Μυστρᾶ, *Πεπραγμένα τοῦ 9ου Διεθνοῦς Βυζαντινολογικοῦ Συνεδρίου*, Thessaloniki, 1955.
DUFRENNE, S., *Les programmes iconographiques des églises byzantines de Mistra*, Paris, 1970.
ZAKYTHINOS, D., *Le despotat grec de la Morée*, v.I., Paris 1932 - v.2, Athens, 1953. (Revised Edition, London, 1975).
LÖHNEYSEN v., F.W., *Mistra, Griechenlands Schicksal im Mittelalter*, Munich 1977.
MASAI, F., *Pléthon et le platonisme de Mistra*, Paris, 1956
MEDVEDEN, I., *Mistra* Leningrad 1973.
MILLET, G., Inscriptions inédites de Mistra, *Bulletin de Correspondance Hellénique*, 1906.
   —*Monuments byzantins de Mistra*, Paris 1910.
   —*Recherches sur l'iconographie de l'Evangile aus XIVe, XVe et XVIe siècles*, Paris, 1916.
   —*L'école grecque dans l'architecture byzantine*, Paris, 1916.
ORLANDOS. A., *Παλάτια καί σπίτια τοῦ Μυστρᾶ*, Athens, 1937.
   —Quelques notes complémentaires sur les maisons paléologuiennes de Mistra, *Art et société à Byzance sous les Paléologues*, Venise, 1971.